Praise for *The Practice of Groundedness*

"This book gets to the heart of the matter."
—Ryan Holiday, author of *Stillness Is the Key* and *Ego Is the Enemy*

"If you ever feel like your own life and the wider world are swirling out of control, you need this book."
—Daniel H. Pink, author of *When*, *Drive*, and *To Sell Is Human*

"Ambitious, far-reaching, and impactful. Stulberg is the writer I turn to for examinations of success in all of its personal and professional complexities."
—David Epstein, author of *Range* and *The Sports Gene*

"This book taps into something that so many of us feel but can't articulate."
—Arianna Huffington, founder and CEO of Thrive Global

"A thoughtful, actionable book for pursuing more excellence with less angst."
—Adam Grant, author of *Think Again* and host of the TED podcast *WorkLife*

"A valuable guide on going from heroic individualism to a more sustainable, long-term vision of success."   —Scott Galloway, author of *The Four* and *Post Corona*

"A crucial alternative for those of us exhausted by soulless exhortations to crush it and looking for a deeper approach to building a successful life."
—Cal Newport, author of *Digital Minimalism* and *Deep Work*

"Exactly what we need at this moment. Stulberg is a master at translating research into strategies to live by."
—Kelly McGonigal, author of *The Willpower Instinct* and *The Joy of Movement*

"Happiness requires a life rooted in values and strengths. But this doesn't happen by itself. Stulberg offers six concrete steps that we can follow that will guide our path."   —Arthur C. Brooks, author of *The Conservative Heart* and *Love Your Enemies*

"A series of down-to-earth prescriptions that teach you to stop fixating on productivity at the expense of well-being. Highly recommend."

—Adam Alter, author of *Irresistible* and *Drunk Tank Pink*

"A wise and beautifully written book. In masterful fashion, Stulberg shows how the bold humility of groundedness is relevant to all aspects of your life. Read it and you'll see."

—Steven C. Hayes, PhD, originator of acceptance and commitment therapy and author of *A Liberated Mind*

"An engaging read with pragmatic tips that can be put into practice right now. This book couldn't come at a better time."

—Judson Brewer, MD, PhD, author of *Unwinding Anxiety* and *The Craving Mind*

THE PRACTICE OF GROUNDEDNESS

A Transformative Path to Success
That Feeds—Not Crushes—Your Soul

BRAD STULBERG

Portfolio/Penguin

Portfolio / Penguin
An imprint of Penguin Random House LLC
penguinrandomhouse.com

Most Portfolio books are available at a discount when purchased
in quantity for sales promotions or corporate use. Special editions,
which include personalized covers, excerpts, and corporate imprints,
can be created when purchased in large quantities. For more
information, please call (212) 572-2232 or e-mail specialmarkets@
penguinrandomhouse.com. Your local bookstore can also assist
with discounted bulk purchases using the Penguin Random House
corporate Business-to-Business program. For assistance in locating
a participating retailer, e-mail B2B@penguinrandomhouse.com.

Library of Congress Cataloging-in-Publication Data
Names: Stulberg, Brad, author.
Title: The practice of groundedness : a transformative path to
success that feeds—not crushes—your soul / Brad Stulberg.
Description: New York : Portfolio/Penguin, [2021] |
Includes bibliographical references and index. |
Identifiers: LCCN 2021000065 (print) | LCCN 2021000066 (ebook) |
ISBN 9780593329894 (hardcover) | ISBN 9780593329900 (ebook)
Subjects: LCSH: Success. | Self-acceptance. |
Self-confidence. | Overachievement.
Classification: LCC BF637.S8 S75 2021 (print) |
LCC BF637.S8 (ebook) | DDC 158.1—dc23
LC record available at https://lccn.loc.gov/2021000065
LC ebook record available at https://lccn.loc.gov/2021000066

Printed in the United States of America
1st Printing

Book design by Alexis Farabaugh

This book stands on the shoulders of giants. Thank you to the scientists, writers, philosophers, poets, saints, monks, and all the other trailblazers whose work this book stands upon. My wish is for this to be a small contribution to an already strong and enduring lineage of thinking and writing.

While working on this book I kept reflecting on how I wanted the outcome to be something that my son, Theo, could be proud of. So this book is for him.

It is also for all of you.

CONTENTS

Part Two

LIVING A GROUNDED LIFE

Part One

THE PRINCIPLES OF GROUNDED SUCCESS

1

GROUNDED TO SOAR

I n the summer of 2019, I began to notice a concerning trend among my coaching clients—high-ranking executives, successful entrepreneurs, physician leaders, and elite athletes. Whereas I used to spend most of my time with them discussing high-performance habits and routines, over the past few years I'd been hearing something else. "I'm dying for a break," said my client Tim, the chief physician of adult and family medicine at a large health care system. "But even when I try to take a single weekend off, I can't seem to go more than a few hours without opening my work email. Logically I know I don't have to—and I don't really want to—but I feel compelled to check. To be honest, I become restless and insecure if I don't."

Other clients experience angst when they don't have the proverbial "next thing" lined up. And even when they do, they worry about falling short. They perceive a deep-seated need to always be pushing toward something, lest they feel a widening gap, a sense of emptiness in their lives. "I thought that when I finally secured funding and launched this business I'd be content," said Samantha, an entrepreneur at a fast-growing technology company. "But I was wrong. And I'm a bit worried that if this isn't enough, I'm not sure what will be."

Some of my clients also report feeling scattered, if not physically then mentally—spending too much time looking back, planning ahead, second-guessing their decisions, or getting caught up in what-if scenarios. "I've long felt the pull of distraction and I've long had a tendency to overthink things," explained Ben, the CEO of a large software company. "Yet it feels intensified now. Like hyper-distraction. It's harder than ever to be present. I can deal with it; but I don't like it."

Most of these individuals—including Tim, Samantha, and Ben—have been go-getters for as long as they can remember. They are determined and goal-driven, and they care deeply about their work and personal lives. They are no strangers to adversity. The athletes have faced awful injuries. The executives who identify as minorities have faced bias and discrimination. The entrepreneurs have stared down arduous hours. Everyone has dealt with significant stress, especially the physicians, who are confronted with life-and-death situations on a regular basis. And yet, despite overcoming these obstacles, all of my clients—individuals whom I've come to admire greatly—continue to struggle mightily.

It's not just my coaching clients. These themes have also been prominent in my research and writing, which has focused on performance, well-being, and general life satisfaction. Many of the people I've gotten to know through this work—top athletes, intellectuals, and creatives—have shared similar discontent. By conventional standards, they are highly successful. But deep down, they, too, often sense that something is not quite right, that something is missing. Interestingly, many of these people tell me that when they aren't wound up they can actually feel quite low. It's not that they are clinically depressed; it's just that they are often bothered by a lingering sense of dissatisfaction. As one world-class athlete reflected to me, "If I stop looking ahead, I start feeling the post-competition blues, even if I won the dang competition! It'd be nice to have a little more, and deeper, peace."

Make no mistake, all of these individuals experience moments of happiness and joy, but the moments are just that: moments—more fleeting than they would like. Too often, they feel like they are being pushed and pulled around by the whims of life, constantly bouncing from one thing to the next, sacrificing autonomy and losing control. They tell themselves (and me) how much they want to turn it off—all of the news and busyness and email and social media notifications and thinking about what's next. And yet when they do, they feel unsettled and restless, fluctuating between aimlessness and angst. They know that always being on isn't the answer, but they never feel quite right when they are off. Many men describe it as a cumbersome need to be bulletproof, invincible. Many women report feeling like they must be everything always, continually falling short of impossible expectations. I've come to call this *heroic individualism*: an ongoing game of one-upmanship, against both yourself and others, paired with the limiting belief that measurable achievement is the only arbiter of success. Even if you do a good job hiding it on the outside, with heroic individualism you chronically feel like you never quite reach the finish line that is lasting fulfillment.

Heroic individualism is not isolated to my coaching, research, or writing. Its woes are a common topic of conversation in my social circle, and those of my younger cousins and older colleagues, too. Regardless of age, race, gender, geography, or line of work, feeling like you are never enough seems to be a significant part of life. This is not exactly new. From the beginning of recorded history, humans have longed to feel like they are solid and whole, even though life is always changing. But the feeling has intensified. Heroic individualism is in the water, perpetuated by a modern culture that relentlessly says you need to be better, feel better, think more positively, have more, and "optimize" your life—only to offer shallow and superficial solutions that, at best, leave you wanting.

If some of this sounds familiar, you are not alone. The details may be different from the examples I've given. Perhaps you dislike your job or have faced acute hardship. Maybe you are fresh out of college or twenty years into your career. Perhaps you are approaching retirement, or even already there. But heroic individualism and its most prevalent symptoms—restlessness, feeling rushed, low-level angst, scatteredness, exhaustion, burnout, periods of emptiness, a compulsion to keep chasing the next thing, and recurrent longing—all of which are supported by mounting data that we'll soon examine, describe what so many people report feeling these days. There are parts of it that describe me, too.

WHEN THE BOTTOM FALLS OUT

My first book, *Peak Performance*, explored the principles required to make sustainable progress in any endeavor. My second book, *The*

Passion Paradox, recognized that some people are wired to keep pushing at all costs, and showed readers how to develop passion and drive and point it in productive directions. I thought the recipe for success and happiness was to cultivate a fruitful passion and then use the principles of *Peak Performance* to channel it, to climb toward mastery. That is certainly how I and so many of my coaching clients had been living our lives—and usually to great triumph. Push, push, push. Go, go, go. Never satisfied. Never enough. Relentless drive and intensity aimed toward whatever is next.

Then, after *Peak Performance* became a bestseller and a complete draft of *The Passion Paradox* was written, I was blindsided by obsessive-compulsive disorder (OCD), a misunderstood and often debilitating disease. Far from a tendency to be overorganized or to double-check things, clinical OCD is characterized by intrusive thoughts and feelings that dominate your life. You spend every waking hour trying to decipher what they mean and how to make them cease, only to have them come back stronger and more violently. They cause electrifying shots of anxiety from head to toe. You compulsively try to distract yourself from them, but they are always there in the background, exploiting any open space in your day. You go to bed with them crawling through your mind and body and you wake up the same way. They are there when you are eating. They are there when you are working. They are there when you are trying to be present for your family. They are even there when you are sleeping, tormenting your dreams. The intrusive thoughts and feelings are so persistent that you start to question whether you might believe them.

In my case, the intrusive thoughts and feelings (obsessions) centered on despair, emptiness, self-harm, and existential distress. Though living with uncontrolled OCD was certainly depressing, deep down I knew I didn't want to hurt myself—but my mind would not leave me alone. It was a chaotic and bottomless spiral of terror. This was my day-to-day reality for the better part a year, before I began to notice the positive effects of therapy and other practices that have changed my work and life for the better.

My OCD wasn't necessarily caused by my ingrained personality traits—a desire to solve every problem, an incessant drive and restlessness, an always-looking-ahead attitude, and an inability to be content. But the diagnosis certainly made me pause and reflect on these qualities. Somehow they seemed linked. As if all of that pushing forward put me in a place where the bottom could more easily fall out. As if OCD was the extreme version of my usual mode of being, only pointed in a dark direction.

THE DANGERS OF RELENTLESS OPTIMIZATION

After I wrote about my experience with OCD in an essay for *Outside* magazine, I received hundreds of notes from readers who also suffered from OCD, anxiety, other mood disorders, or a generalized sense of unease. Many of them expressed that they, too, had an insatiable drive that, prior to the onset of their disorders, was celebrated. That drive and forward energy had helped them accomplish great things. It was a source of excitement. But now, like me, they found themselves wondering if their inability to be content and their outsize focus on growth and progress—on more, more, more, on always pushing forward—somehow contributed to a mind in pathological overdrive; a mind that couldn't downshift; a mind that couldn't find its ground.

These notes made me realize that we do everything we can to optimize our entire existence so we can finally feel like we are enough. But perhaps this isn't so optimal. In ancient Eastern psychology there is a concept known as the hungry ghost. The hungry ghost has a bottomless stomach. He keeps on eating, stuffing himself sick, but he never feels full. It's a severe disorder, and one many people still experience.

The groundbreaking sociologist Émile Durkheim noted that "Overweening ambition always exceeds the results obtained, great as they may be, since there is no wanting to pause here. Nothing gives satisfaction and all this agitation is uninterruptedly maintained without appeasement. . . . How could [mental health] not be weakened under such conditions?" Though the following afflictions do not exist in a vacuum, many appear to be related to heroic individualism, if not a direct by-product of it. Rates of clinical anxiety and depression are higher than ever, with estimates showing more than one in five people are suffering at any given time. Addictions to harmful substances are at peak levels in modern history, as evidenced by increasing rates of alcoholism and the opioid epidemic. There has been a tragic rise in what researchers call *deaths of despair*, or fatalities caused by drugs, alcohol, or suicide. In 2017, the most recent year for which we have data as of this writing, more than 150,000 Americans experienced deaths of despair. That is the highest this number has ever been, and nearly twice as high as it was in 1999.

According to the latest research in cognitive science, psychology, organizational behavior, medicine, and sociology, large swaths of people are struggling with feelings of dissatisfaction, too.

Research from Gallup, a large polling organization, shows that overall well-being and life satisfaction in the United States are down nearly 10 percent since 2008. The data "suggests a trend that not all is well with people in the United States," summarizes *The American Journal of Managed Care*. The reasons for this are manifold. Even prior to the COVID-19 pandemic, fewer people were engaging in traditional community gathering places than at any point in recent history. Political tribalism is rising. At the same time, experts believe that loneliness and social isolation have reached epidemic proportions. In 2019, the World Health Organization classified burnout as a medical condition, defining it as "chronic workplace stress that has not been successfully managed." Insomnia is more common than ever, as is chronic pain. When you put all of this together, it seems safe to say that people's underlying feelings of not being or having enough are increasingly surfacing. The irony is that so many of the people experiencing these afflictions are productive and successful, at least by conventional standards. But surely this isn't the kind of success they are after.

Signs You May Be Suffering from Heroic Individualism

These feelings can manifest in different ways, but the concerns I have heard most frequently include the following:

- Low-level anxiety and a sensation of always being rushed or in a hurry—if not physically, then mentally

- A sense that your life is swirling with frenetic energy, as if you're being pushed and pulled from one thing to the next

- A recurring intuition that something isn't quite right, but you're unsure what that something is, let alone what to do about it

- Not always wanting to be on, but struggling to turn off and not feeling good when you do

- Feeling way too busy, but also restless when you have open time and space

- Being easily distractible and unable to focus, struggling to sit in silence without reaching for your phone

- Wanting to do better, be better, and feel better, but having no idea where to start

- Becoming utterly overwhelmed by the information, products, and competing claims on what leads to well-being, self-improvement, and performance

- Feeling lonely or empty inside

- Struggling to be content

- Being successful by conventional standards, yet feeling like you're never enough

This cluster of characteristics represents a common mode of being in today's world. It may even be the prevailing one. But as you'll see in the coming pages, it doesn't have to be.

ENTER GROUNDEDNESS, A BETTER WAY

All of this was on my mind during a hike with my close friend Mario. Both of us were going through our own respective rough patch, feeling more unsettled than we'd like. It was a crisp and windy day with a light gray sky. The upper branches of the massive California redwood trees were blowing violently, but hundreds of feet below, the trees weren't moving at all. Their trunks were rock solid, held to the ground by a network of strong and interconnected roots. And that's when the lightbulb went off. I remember looking at Mario and saying, *That's it. This is what we're missing. This is what we need to be developing. We need to stop spending so much time worrying about our metaphorical overstory, our high-hanging branches, and instead focus on nourishing our deep and internal roots. The stuff that keeps us grounded throughout all kinds of weather. The foundation. The principles and practices that we often overlook, that get crowded out in a too-busy life focused on the relentless and all-too-often single-minded pursuit of outward achievement.*

At that moment I realized what I was longing for, what Mario was longing for, what my coaching clients and the elite performers I write about are longing for, and what I'm pretty sure everyone is longing for: to feel grounded—and to experience a deeper and more fulfilling kind of success as a result.

Groundedness is unwavering internal strength and self-confidence that sustains you through ups and downs. It is a deep reservoir of integrity and fortitude, of wholeness, out of which lasting performance, well-being, and fulfillment emerge. Yet here's the common trap: when you become too focused on productivity, optimization, growth, and the latest bright and shiny objects, you neglect your ground. Eventually, you end up suffering. Conversely, and this is something that this book will unpack in great detail, when you prioritize groundedness, you do not neglect passion, performance, or productivity. Nor does groundedness eliminate all forms of ambition. Rather, it situates and stabilizes these qualities, so that your striving and ambition become less frenetic and more focused, sustainable, and fulfilling; less about achieving something out in front of you and more about living in alignment with your innermost values, pursuing your interests, and expressing your authentic self in the here and now, and in a manner you can be proud of. When you are grounded there is no need to look up or down. You are where you are, and you hold true strength and power from that position. The success you experience becomes more enduring and robust. It is only once you are grounded that you can truly soar, at least in a sustainable manner.

What, then, would it look like if instead of always pushing for conventional success, you focused on cultivating groundedness? What if the answer is less about excitement for the future and more about leaning into the present? What if you stopped trying so damn hard to be great all the time, stopped focusing on external results, and instead focused on laying down a solid foundation—a kind of groundedness that is not an outcome or a onetime event, but a way of being? A groundedness out of which peak performance *and* well-being and fulfillment can emerge and prevail for a lifetime? How would one develop this kind of powerful groundedness that is not so susceptible to the changing weather patterns of our lives? Might there be a way to be more at ease and content, more solid and whole, and still perform to the utmost of your potential?

To answer these questions, I looked to scientific research, ancient wisdom, and modern practice.

WHAT SCIENTIFIC RESEARCH HAS TO SAY

Studies show that happiness is a function of reality minus expectations. In other words, the key to being happy isn't to always want and strive for more. Instead, happiness is found in the present moment, in creating a meaningful life and being fully engaged in it, right here and right now. There is no doubt that meeting one's basic needs—such as shelter, food, and health care—is critical to any definition of happiness or well-being. Without those elements in place, little else is possible. While some studies show income is correlated with well-being and happiness, other research, such as that conducted by the Nobel Prize–winning psychologist Daniel Kahneman, shows that above a certain threshold, somewhere between $65,000 and $80,000 per year, perhaps with minor adjustments for geography, additional household income is not associated with additional happiness or well-being. Even if it may be a factor, it is not the driving force.

What's more, we're all affected by what behavioral scientists call *hedonic adaptation*, or the "set-point" theory of happiness: when we acquire or achieve something new, our happiness, well-being, and satisfaction rise, but only for a few months before returning to their prior levels. This is precisely why it is so hard, if not impossible, to outwardly achieve your way out of heroic individualism. If anything, thinking that you can is the crux of heroic individualism's trap.

Speaking about the common struggle to find enduring happiness and well-being, Harvard psychologist Tal Ben-Shahar, who coined the term "arrival fallacy," says, "We live under the illusion—well, the false hope—that once we make it, then we'll be happy." But when we do make it, when we finally "arrive," he says, we may feel a temporary blip of happiness, but that feeling doesn't last. And this is to say nothing of all the times we don't make it, when we suffer the inevitable setbacks that life brings. Ben-Shahar says that if the cycle of seeking happiness outside ourselves and failing to find it repeats enough, eventually we lose hope. But this doesn't have to be the case. As this book will show, there is a way to change your set point—to permanently increase your happiness, well-being, satisfaction, and performance—that has nothing to do with focusing on external achievement or chasing status. Rather, it has to do with focusing on groundedness.

In clinical psychology, acceptance and commitment therapy (ACT), cognitive behavioral therapy (CBT), and dialectical behavior therapy (DBT) are three of the most effective methods to improve anxiety, mood, and self-confidence. Common to all of these therapies is the belief that happiness, stability, and equanimity emerge from being grounded. These therapies are generally used only for recovery from serious mental health issues and addiction, but that's unfortunate. As you'll learn in the chapters ahead, their approaches and the practices they teach can be enormously beneficial for everyone, from everyday people to world-class performers.

Meanwhile, the emerging field of performance science is revealing that any kind of lasting success requires a solid base of health, well-being, and general life satisfaction. Without this foundation, someone can perform well for a short period of time, but they inevitably break down and burn out, and usually after only a few years at most. A common attribute in high performers who struggle with injury and illness—both physical and emotional—is that they neglect groundedness in favor of always pushing forward. Individuals who prioritize taking care of their ground, however, tend to have long, fulfilling, and successful careers. This theme is apparent in diverse fields, from athletics to creativity to business to medicine.

Finally, decades of research on motivation and burnout shows that striving toward a goal is most sustainable and fulfilling when your drive comes from deep within. Not from the need—or for some, the addiction, and a hard one to shake—to receive external validation.

WHAT ANCIENT WISDOM HAS TO SAY

Nearly all of the world's ancient wisdom traditions emphasize the importance of cultivating groundedness. Once practitioners develop this refuge—an intimate sense of strength and stability, of deep and heartfelt self-confidence, of belonging to themselves—they are less prone to getting caught up in fleeting desires or becoming overwhelmed by the daily challenges of life.

Buddhism, Stoicism, Taoism, and other ancient wisdom traditions have been teaching this lesson for millennia. The Buddha taught that the only place true peace can be found is in our "loving awareness"—or what Westerners might call the soul, the part of us that rests underneath all the busyness and content of daily life, our enduring and essential nature that is unfazed by external comings and goings. Buddhism also teaches a concept called "right effort," which states that when one's striving is grounded, it leads to more meaningful contribution, satisfaction, and fulfillment. The Stoics believed that in order to have a good life, we must shift from trying to attain status or the approval of others, both of which are fleeting, and focus on becoming "properly grounded," relinquishing the need to look outside ourselves for satisfaction and fulfillment and instead finding it within. The well-known Taoist philosopher Lao-tzu taught that the wind of the world ebbs and flows, but if you learn to hold your ground you can maintain balance regardless of what is happening around you. The fourth-century Christian theologian Saint Augustine acknowledged the human propensity to crave worldly achievements, but, foreshadowing the arrival fallacy, he warned that if you become a slave to outward ambition you'll be forever dissatisfied, always chasing the next best thing, always getting caught up in the ephemeral and fleeting, always looking for love in all the wrong places. Later on, the thirteenth-century Christian mystic Meister Eckhart's teachings focused on developing an unshakable groundedness out of which authentic actions arise. "Interiority turns into effective action and effective action leads back to interiority and we become used to acting without any compulsion," Eckhart said. "The deeper and lower the ground, the higher and more immeasurable is the elevation and the height."

The recurring theme is clear: if you want to do well and be well in an enduring manner, you need to be grounded. What's interesting, and something I'll discuss more in later chapters, is that not one of these ancient wisdom traditions promotes passivity. They all promote *wise action*. Wise action is very different from our default mode of *reaction*. Whereas reaction is rushed and rash, wise action is deliberate and considerate. Wise action emerges from internal strength, from groundedness.

WHAT MODERN PRACTITIONERS OF GROUNDEDNESS HAVE TO TEACH US

When I looked at the world's best and most fulfilled performers I found that they, too, focus on nurturing their groundedness. Consider the Dark Horse Project, a long-term study out of Harvard University that explores how men and women across diverse and often unusual fields—from musicians to dog trainers to writers to sommeliers to hot-air balloon pilots—develop unique processes to achieve their own, personal versions of peak performance, and more important, fulfillment and life satisfaction. The findings, which were published in the book *Dark Horse*, written by human-development researcher Todd Rose and neuroscientist Ogi Ogas, center around two major themes followed by people who chart untraditional paths to good lives: these "dark horses" focus on accomplishing the things that matter most to them, and they don't compare themselves to others or to conventional definitions of success.

"The first thing is actually knowing yourself," says Rose. "For most of us, when we think about who we are, we often talk about what we're good at or the job we do. . . . And what we found in dark horses is that they focus incredibly on what matters to them and what motivates them, and use that as a basis for their identity. And I think that when you anchor around what truly motivates you, that is getting you on the path of fulfillment."

It can also be instructive to study the experiences of other world-class performers who suffered from distress, saw their performance plummet, but then bounced back. These include people like two-time Olympian and endurance athlete Sarah True, musician Sara Bareilles, basketball stars Kevin Love and DeMar DeRozan, *Full House* actress Andrea Barber, and trailblazing scientist Steven Hayes. As you'll read in the coming pages, they all struggled with periods of heroic individualism and related burnout, anxiety, and depression. Their lows had at least one thing in common: they tended to follow periods of getting overly caught up in striving and chasing after conventional success. It was only when they returned to nurturing their groundedness that they felt better—and began performing better, too.

THE PRINCIPLES OF GROUNDEDNESS

A guiding tenet in my work—both as a writer and as a coach—is pattern recognition. I'm not interested in "hacks," quick fixes, or single small studies, all of which tend to be big on promises but low on real-world efficacy. Regardless of what the marketers, click-bait headlines, and pseudoscience evangelists say, there are no magic lotions, potions, or pills when it comes to deep happiness, lasting well-being, and enduring performance.

What I am interested in is convergence. If multiple fields of scientific inquiry, the world's major wisdom traditions, and the practices of highly fulfilled peak performers all point toward the same truths, then they are probably worth paying attention to. In this instance, happiness, fulfillment, well-being, and sustainable performance arise when you concentrate on being present in the process of living instead of obsessing over outcomes, and above all when you're firmly grounded wherever you are.

The remainder of this book is my attempt to figure out how to live this truth. First, I will unpack the essential, evidence-based principles of groundedness where there is clear convergence between modern science, ancient wisdom, and the experience of happy, healthy, high-performing people. Out of a commitment to these principles—acceptance, presence, patience, vulnerability, deep community, and movement—comes a firm and resolute groundedness. Briefly, the six principles of groundedness are as follows:

- *Accept* **Where You Are to Get You Where You Want to Go.** Seeing clearly, accepting, and starting where you are. Not where you want to be. Not where you think you should be. Not where other people think you should be. But where you are.

- **Be *Present* So You Can Own Your Attention and Energy.** Being present, both physically and mentally, for what is in front of you. Spending more time fully in *this* life, not in thoughts about the past or future.

- **Be *Patient* and You'll Get There Faster.** Giving things time and space to unfold. Not trying to escape life by moving at warp speed. Not expecting instant results and then quitting when they don't occur. Shifting from being a seeker to a practitioner. Playing the long game. Staying on the path instead of constantly veering off.

- **Embrace *Vulnerability* to Develop Genuine Strength and Confidence.** Showing up authentically. Being real with yourself and with others. Eliminating the cognitive dissonance between your workplace self, your online self, and your actual self so that you can know and trust your true self, and in turn gain the freedom and confidence to devote your energy to what matters most.

- **Build *Deep Community*.** Nurturing genuine connection and belonging. Prioritizing not just productivity, but people, too. Immersing yourself in supportive spaces that will hold and bolster you through ups and downs, and that will give you the chance to do the same for others.

- ***Move* Your Body to Ground Your Mind.** Regularly moving your body so that you fully inhabit it, connect it to your mind, and as a result become more firmly situated wherever you are.

For each principle, we'll explore the wide-ranging, cross-discipline evidence behind it. We'll see how all these principles support one another, like the roots that hold a towering redwood tree to the ground. We'll also examine an interesting paradox: why letting go of—or at least holding more lightly—outcomes such as happiness and achievement, and instead focusing on building a durable foundation of groundedness, is the surest path to becoming happier and more successful.

CLOSING THE KNOWING-DOING GAP

While the concepts and ideas in this book ought to have a positive impact on your mindset, you will realize their full power only when you apply them. This is why you'll not only learn about the principles of groundedness but also find concrete and evidence-based practices for taking them off these pages and making them real. In my work with coaching clients, I call this the *knowing-doing* gap. First, you need to understand something and be convinced of its value. Then, you actually need to do it. The remaining chapters are structured in this way, with a detailed examination of each principle, followed by concrete practices to enact it.

It is worth recognizing, however, that the principles of groundedness don't just go against societal norms, but they may also go against your personal habit energy, your past ways of being and doing. Though you may sense that many of your habitual ways are counterproductive, you may still struggle to change them. This is normal. Change is a challenge. The inertia of what you've always done is real—and it can be quite strong. As you'll see throughout this book, living a grounded life is an ongoing practice.

It's one thing to understand something intellectually. It's another to make it real, day in and day out. As the Zen master Thich

Nhat Hanh says, "If you want to garden, you have to bend down and touch the soil. Gardening is a practice. Not an idea."

The time to start nourishing a solid and steadfast groundedness is now. We'll start with the first principle, learning what it means to accept where you are and seeing why it's the key to getting where you want to go.

2

ACCEPT WHERE YOU ARE TO GET YOU WHERE YOU WANT TO GO

August 2016. It was a hot day in Rio de Janeiro, Brazil. The setting was Fort Copacabana, a military base on the edge of the South Atlantic Ocean. The world's best triathletes were about to plunge into the water, beginning a race in which they'd swim, bike, and run for Olympic glory. One of the three female athletes representing the United States was named Sarah True.

This wasn't True's first rodeo. In the 2012 Games, she finished fourth, a painful ten seconds off the podium and a medal. Not only was True determined to take care of unfinished business in 2016, but she was also racing for her husband, Ben True—a world-class endurance athlete in his own right, one of the best middle-distance runners the United States has ever produced. However, the Olympics had always eluded him. Ben was hopeful that his single-minded dedication to training would pay off in 2016, but, during the preliminary trials, he failed to make the Olympic team by less than one second. For a couple to devote their entire lives to the pursuit of excellence and come so devastatingly close to achieving their goals but ultimately falling seconds short—and not once, but twice—that hurts.

So, as Sarah True jumped off the dock at Copacabana and into the ocean, she was carrying double the load. "Whether we liked it or not," she reflected to me, "*our* Olympic experience had become *my* Olympic experience."

True swam well, as she always does, putting herself in a position to compete for gold. But as she pulled herself onto land and charged toward her bike, her leg began to spasm. She assumed her muscles were tight and once she started riding they would relax. But they never did. True struggled on the bike, pedaled onward with a sullen grimace for as long as she could. Eventually, she dropped out of the race altogether. "My body failed me," she says. It was as simple and as hard—and oh, was it hard—as that.

True did what she could to hold her head up high, but it was an act. She was devastated. It wasn't long after the flight from Brazil touched down in the States that True began to spiral into a deep and dark depression. "I could only manage about four hours of sleep per night, and that was with the use of prescription sleep aids and pain medication," she remembers. "I failed Ben. I failed myself. There is no point to any of this," she thought.

True did what any hard-nosed endurance athlete would. She tried to push through the pain. She told herself it would pass. That she could bear it out. Unfortunately, she was wrong. Even her foolproof numbing mechanism, hours-long bike rides, didn't work. "I obsessively thought about taking my own life," she told me. "I'd be on long training rides and I could not stop thinking about swerving into oncoming traffic. Every truck became an object that could end it all."

Her spiral continued into 2017. Month after month passed and True kept thinking that her depression could not possibly get any worse. And yet it just kept getting worse.

Finally, in mid-2017, True opened up to what was happening and fully accepted the enormity of her grief and subsequent depression. She stopped resisting it, trying to fight it alone, and began intensive therapy. When I asked her to think back, she couldn't pinpoint a single day, event, or reason that prompted her to seek help. More than anything, she was tired, and she was still alive. "Endurance athletes are taught to endure, to keep pressing on," she told me. "When something isn't right you just push harder; you press on, you keep going. But clearly, that mindset was not going to work here."

True, who had been struggling with depression on and off since high school, explained that she realized there would never be a good time to step back from her life in order to confront her illness in all of its entirety. But, she explained, now it was raging, and she realized that she was living on a fragile foundation, if on any foundation at all. She couldn't stand going on like this. For True, far more challenging than pushing ahead in even the most grueling triathlon race was slowing down, accepting where she was, and confronting and working through her depression and its causes—neither of which she was particularly excited about confronting or working through.

MOVING FORWARD REQUIRES ACCEPTING WHERE YOU ARE

Though perhaps not publicly or to the same extent, like Sarah True, we have all experienced highs and lows, both professionally and personally. Life is not easy. Things don't always go our way. The human condition is a messy one. Much more is outside our control than we wish: aging, illness, mortality, the economy, the actions of people we care about, to name just a few. This can be a hard, and at times scary, reality to accept.

Instead of accepting this truth, when things don't go our way we tend to default to magical thinking, convincing ourselves we're in a better place than we are. Social scientists call this *motivated reasoning*, or our propensity *not* to see things clearly but instead to reason our way into seeing things as we'd like them to be. A common example of motivated reasoning is when you know that you no longer want to be in a job you dislike, but instead of facing that uncomfortable truth, you look for (and find) numerous reasons why your current job—the one you can't stand—is actually great. Or, even easier, we ignore our stressors altogether. We bury our heads in the sand or do precisely what society's heroic individualism and superficial success culture tell us to do: think positive thoughts, numb and distract ourselves, buy stuff and tweet. We engage in frantic and compulsory activity to distract ourselves from our problems and fears. We expect things to get better without ever acknowledging or accepting our true starting point. Though this may save us some short-term pain, it's not a good long-term solution. That's because we groove into a pattern of not addressing the thing that actually needs addressing—whether it be unhealthy habits, loneliness in a relationship, burnout in the workplace, a mind-body system that is on edge, or a community on the brink of unrest. The result is that we never feel fully grounded where we are—because we're never really living our full reality.

The first principle of groundedness is *acceptance.* Progress in anything, large or small, requires recognizing, accepting, and starting where you are. Not where you want to be. Not where you think you should be. Not where others think you should be. But where you are. As you'll soon see, acceptance is key to happiness and performance in the now, and also to productive change in the future. The pioneering humanistic psychologist Carl Rogers spent decades working with individuals on personal growth and fulfillment. Perhaps his most poignant observation, the one he became most known for: "The curious paradox is that when I accept myself just as I am, then I can change."

When you first hear acceptance you may think of giving up, complacency, phoning it in, or committing to mediocrity. But this isn't the case. Acceptance is not passive resignation. Acceptance is taking stock of a situation and seeing it clearly for what it is—whether you like it or not. It is only once you gain a clear understanding of a situation, and get at least comfortable enough being in it, that you can take wise and productive action to get where you want to go.

My own acceptance story began during my recovery from OCD, but now I do my best to apply this principle in all areas of my life, and with my coaching clients too. Prior to the onset of OCD, I tended to deal with challenges by denying them, resisting them, ignoring them, or most commonly, trying to problem-solve my way out of them. These tactics worked well enough when I got cut from the high school basketball team, got dumped by the college girlfriend I thought I'd marry, didn't get the job I wanted, lost potential clients, and had my writing rejected. OCD, however, is a different animal.

Nonstop thoughts, feelings of dread and despair, and urges to self-harm are bad enough when you have a reason to feel them. They are even worse when you don't. The latter is typical of OCD, and when its violent storm hit me—when my wife was pregnant with our first child, one of the worst possible times for something like this to happen—I did the only thing I knew how to do. First, I denied it altogether, telling myself it was some kind of mysterious physical ailment that would pass, perhaps some sort of virus that was affecting my mind. Then, I resisted and problem-solved. I tried endlessly to make the thoughts, feelings, and urges go away. I kept telling myself some version of: *This is a nightmare; it's not really happening. After all, I am an "expert" and coach on mental skills and performance. There must be a way I can will myself better.* Wrong. Wrong. And wrong again. My refusal to accept my situation and my resistance to it not only were futile but also made matters worse. The more I pushed against my experience of OCD, the stronger it became. Trying to suppress my intrusive thoughts, feelings, and urges—or distract myself from them altogether—had the opposite effect. It fueled their fire.

Finally, with the help of a kind, compassionate, and skilled therapist, I began to surrender. I accepted the fact that I was sick; that these thoughts, feelings, and urges were real, and they were not going to disappear overnight. I couldn't problem-solve my way out over the course of a couple of hours, or even days. I had to learn to do what was—and on some days still is—the hardest work of my life: accept the ugly thoughts, feelings, and urges and let them be there. As I was coming to terms with this my therapist would tell me that I didn't need to like OCD, but I needed to embrace it. At the very least, I had to see it clearly for what it was. I had to learn to stop resisting reality and wanting things to be different. Instead, I had to be with what was happening, even, and perhaps especially, if I couldn't stand it. This was the first real step in my recovery. Only when I acknowledged and accepted the very thing I wanted neither to acknowledge nor to accept could I start taking actions that would make my situation better. You can't work on something in a meaningful way if you are fighting it at the same time. And even upstream of that, you can't work on something in a meaningful way if you refuse to accept that the thing is happening to begin with. Far too often we focus on the acute challenges of our lives without realizing, accepting, and addressing their distal causes.

ACCEPTANCE AND HAPPINESS

The gap between wishful thinking and reality not only precludes you from taking productive actions to improve your situation in the future but also causes dissatisfaction in the here and now. In 2006, epidemiologists from the University of Southern Denmark set out to explore why their citizens consistently score higher than any other Western country on measures of happiness and life satisfaction. Their findings, which were published in *The BMJ*, focused on the importance of expectations. "If expectations are unrealistically high they could be the basis of disappointment and low life satisfaction," write the authors. "While the Danes are very satis-fied, their expectations are rather low."

In a 2014 study, researchers from the University College London examined people's happiness from moment to moment. They found that "momentary happiness in response to outcomes of a probabilistic reward task is not explained by current task earnings, but by the combined influence of the recent reward expectations and prediction errors arising from those expectations." In lay terms, happiness at any given moment equals reality minus expectations. If your expectations are constantly higher than your reality, you'll never be content. Jason Fried, founder and CEO of the successful software company Basecamp, who has written multiple articles on professional satisfaction, put it like this: "I used to set up expectations in my head all day long. Constantly measuring reality against an imagined reality is taxing and tiring. I think it often wrings the joy out of just experiencing something for what it is."

The message here isn't necessarily to always set low expectations. Pushing for more and pursuing just-manageable challenges is integral to growth and fulfillment. It's okay, even admirable, to set a high bar, but—and this is a big but—you need to be present and accepting as you strive. Instead of wanting things to be different and then being disappointed when they are not, you need to be with your reality as it is, not just for the highs but for the lows too. Only then can you take wise action to bring about the kind of change that you desire. It's kind of like this: desperately trying to be happy or successful is one of the worst ways to actually be happy or successful.

Long before the aforementioned studies were completed, Joseph Campbell, one of the world's foremost experts on mythology and *actual* heroism, wrote, "The crux of the curious difficulty for the hero lies in the fact that our conscious views of what life *ought* to be seldom correspond to what life really is." During his decades of research, Campbell observed that, in stories spanning cultures and traditions, at some point on their journey the mythical hero must close the gap between their reality and their expectations. Generally, the hero-to-be gets stuck resisting their reality for quite some time. Eventually, however, they learn to confront and overcome this difficulty; in essence, they learn to practice acceptance. This opens the door for their taking strong and appropriate action—for their becoming a hero.

Far from the frantic and reactive activity we so often engage in with heroic individualism, we can be more like Campbell's heroes, learning to practice acceptance and take wise action throughout our lives, even amid difficulty. Fortunately, there is an established method to help, and it's backed by nearly forty years of research and more than a thousand scientific studies.

ACCEPTANCE AND COMMITMENT

Steven Hayes is a clinical psychologist and professor at the University of Nevada, Reno. He's written forty-four books, has advised countless PhD students, and is one of the fifteen hundred most cited scholars in the world, living or dead. He is inarguably among the most influential clinical psychologists of our time. Hayes's own hero's journey came to a head in 1982, at two in the morning on a brown-and-gold shag carpet in a second-story, one-bedroom apartment that he shared with his then-girlfriend in Greensboro, North Carolina.

For three years, Hayes told me, he had been "spiraling down into the hell that is panic disorder." For a newly minted PhD in psychology, this was particularly distressing and disorienting. Hayes was supposed to have it together, but he would experience overwhelming anxiety in department meetings. Eventually, the anxiety encroached upon his personal life, affecting him while out with friends, exercising, and ultimately even at home. On one particular night in 1982, Hayes awoke with what he describes as a monster panic attack. His heart was pounding. He could feel his pulse in his neck, forehead, and arms. His chest was tightening. His arms were cramping. He was struggling to breathe.

"I wanted to call 911. I thought I was having a heart attack," he recalled to me. "Yes, I was aware of my panic disorder. And yes, as a psychologist I knew full well that these were the symptoms of my own personal variety of panic, but my brain kept telling me that this was different. This was the real thing, the real McCoy." Hayes wanted desperately to run, fight, hide—anything but to be where he was. He remembers thinking that there was no way he could drive in his condition, so he'd better call an ambulance. "Make the call, have them get the emergency room prepared, make the damn call, Steven, you're dying. . . . That's what I was thinking," he told me. But he didn't make the call. Instead, Hayes remembers having what he refers to as "an out-of-body experience," gaining space between what was happening and his awareness of what was happening—no longer being in the situation but viewing it from afar. In this space, Hayes imagined what would happen if he called an ambulance. "They'd rush me to the hospital. They'd hook me up to tubes and devices. And then, the doctor, a young man with a smirk on his face, would walk into the room and say, 'Steve, you're not having a heart attack. You're just having a panic attack.'" Hayes knew it was true. "This was just another level down in hell," he said. "Rock bottom."

But this time around, Hayes bounced back, and another path emerged. It led to a deep and rarely visited internal part of him. He remembers this part of him saying, *I don't know who you are, but apparently you can make me hurt. You can make me suffer. But I'll tell you one thing you cannot do. You cannot make me turn away from my own experience.* And with that, Hayes stood up. He looked down at the brown-and-gold shag carpet and promised that never again would he run from himself or his circumstances. "I didn't know how to keep that promise," he told me, "and I had no idea how I would bring that promise into the lives of others. But I knew I would. I was done running away."

Hayes emerged from his harrowing experience dedicated to understanding what had happened and how he could apply it—not only to help himself but also to help others. This set in motion a four-decade scientific exploration. Through hundreds of experiments, Hayes learned that the more someone tries to avoid unpleasant circumstances, thoughts, feelings, and urges—exactly what Hayes had been doing before his insight on that fateful night—the stronger and more frequent they become. "If you cannot open up to discomfort without suppression," he says, "it becomes impossible to face difficult problems in a healthy way."

Hayes's work spawned a therapeutic model called acceptance and commitment therapy, or ACT for short. In a nutshell, ACT suggests that when you're in a difficult or scary situation—be it physical, emotional, or social—resisting it almost always makes it worse. Far better is to accept what is happening; to open yourself up to it, feel it deeply, and let it be there. And then you've got to commit to living your life in alignment with your innermost values anyway. You feel what is. You accept what is. You see clearly what is. And instead of running away from what is, you carry it with you and take productive action.

An integral part of ACT is giving yourself permission to *not* always have everything together. It's about allowing yourself to feel pain and hurt and unease and greed and anger and jealousy and sadness and insecurity and emptiness and all the other unpleasant emotions that are core to our species, even though our culture's heroic individualism falsely signals you shouldn't. An ancient Buddhist teaching states that everyone in life will experience ten thousand joys and ten thousand sorrows. If you never accept the darkness inherent in the human condition you'll never find lasting joy. This is because whenever unpleasant experiences or situations arise, you'll only want them to go away. But, as Hayes's work and my own experience with OCD show, it is this very resistance that makes them stickier and stronger, and thus more entrenched. Instead of denying your reality, pretending certain circumstances are otherwise, you must learn to accept it and see it clearly.

The objective of ACT is not the elimination of difficulties. Rather, it is to be present with whatever life throws your way and to move in the direction of your values, even if doing so feels hard in the moment. Though the research of Hayes and his colleagues— experiments showing that ACT dramatically improves depression, anxiety, OCD, burnout, and even performance—is groundbreaking, the premise of ACT is not exactly new. Hayes will be the first to tell you that in many ways, his modern science is merely providing empirical support for age-old wisdom.

The most powerful teachings of ACT, which I'll detail later in the chapter, can be distilled into a three-part process, which happens to fit into the acronym ACT:

1. **A**ccept what is happening without fusing your identity to it. Zoom out to a larger perspective or awareness from which you can observe your situation without feeling like you are trapped in it.

2. **C**hoose how you want to move forward in a way that aligns with your innermost values.

3. **T**ake action, even if doing so feels scary or uncomfortable.

THE WISDOM OF ACCEPTANCE: DON'T LET THE ARROW HIT YOU TWICE

More than two thousand years ago, in his journal of meditations, the Stoic emperor Marcus Aurelius wrote, "It's normal to feel pain in your hands and feet if you're using your feet as feet and your hands as hands. And for a human being to feel stress is normal—if he's living a normal human life." Epictetus, another revered Stoic, taught that when we hate or fear our circumstances, they become our masters. Contrary to modern times, where the cult of positive thinking dominates and we're bombarded with messages like, *If you're not always happy and crushing it, then you're doing it wrong*, the Stoics had a more honest and psychologically sound view of life. It's completely normal to feel stress. It's completely normal to find ourselves in unappealing circumstances. This doesn't mean you are broken. It means you are human. The more you fear, deny, or resist problems, pain, and difficult circumstances—from minor annoyances to major disturbances—the worse off you'll be. The more you focus on what you can control and cease worrying about what you cannot, the better.

Around the same time the Stoics were writing about acceptance in Greece and Rome, across the world in India and Southeast Asia the Buddhists were coming to similar conclusions. An elegant Buddhist parable teaches not to let the arrow hit you twice. The first arrow—be it a negative thought, feeling, event, or circumstance—you can't always control. But you can control the second arrow, or your reaction to the first one. Often, this reaction is one of denial, suppression, judgment, resistance, or impulsive action—all of which tend to create more, not less, difficulty and distress. The Buddha taught that it is this, the second arrow, that hurts worse, and it is also the second arrow that prevents you from doing anything wise about the first one.

The idea of the second arrow runs deep in Buddhist teachings. The legend goes that on the eve of his awakening, the Buddha was assaulted by the god Mara, who represents fear, craving, suffering, anger, delusion, and a host of other maladies. Throughout the night, Mara levied upon the Buddha storms, armies, and demons. He assaulted the Buddha with arrows of greed, hatred, jealousy, and delusion. Yet instead of resisting these arrows, the Buddha met each one with a present, tender, and spacious awareness. As he did, the arrows were transformed into flowers. Over time, the petals piled up into a mound, and the Buddha became increasingly calm and clear. Mara kept on assaulting the Buddha, and the Buddha kept on responding with acceptance and compassion. Eventually, Mara realized the Buddha would not resist or suppress his attacks, and he retreated. It is in this way that the Buddha became enlightened. He could finally see clearly and fully. He could stand firmly grounded, regardless of the arrows that were coming his way.

Mara was not a onetime visitor, but appears repeatedly throughout ancient Buddhist texts. Each time the Buddha is confronted with Mara, instead of being lured into a cycle of denial, delusion, and suffering, the Buddha simply says, "I see you, Mara," and then proceeds to accept what is happening and take wise action, a clear expression of unshakable groundedness. In her book *Radical Acceptance*, the psychologist and Buddhist scholar Tara Brach writes, "Just as the Buddha willingly opened himself up to an encounter with Mara, we too can pause and make ourselves available to whatever life is offering us in each moment." We, too, can turn the arrows of suffering into flowers, or at least soften their edges, and in doing so gain a sense of unwavering groundedness.

This approach may run counter to habitual ways of being and doing, particularly for those of us who grew up in a Western society. We're programmed to react to circumstances, take control of our situations, try to force positive thoughts, and immediately jump into problem solving. But it's the step of acceptance that makes all of these other strategies effective. Without acceptance, we risk running around in circles, not really working on the things we need to be working on, never making progress. Not accepting our reality causes us to feel tenuous and unsteady, like we're never really on solid ground. It prevents us from achieving our potential, too.

ACCEPTANCE AND PEAK PERFORMANCE GO HAND IN HAND

Conventional wisdom states that if you want to be a peak performer, you must always be hungry and pushing, never satisfied or content. But as is usually the case with inspirational axioms, the truth is a bit more complicated. Something I discuss often with my coaching clients is the difference between performing from a place of freedom and love and performing from a place of constriction and fear. The former happens when you accept where you are; when you trust your training, have realistic expectations, and stay within yourself. When you are grounded. The latter happens when you question, deny, or resist your reality; when you feel the need, or in some cases the compulsion, to be somewhere or something you are not.

When you lie to yourself about your situation, doubt and anxiety almost always ensue. You go from playing to win to playing not to lose. Psychologists call this the difference between a performance-approach and a performance-avoidance mindset. When you adopt a performance-approach mindset, you are playing to win, focusing on the potential rewards of success. You have an easier time immersing yourself in the moment and entering a flowlike state. Under a performance-avoidance mindset, however, your focus is on dodging mistakes and circumventing danger. You are constantly on the lookout for threats and problems because deep down you know that you don't belong.

Research out of the University of Kent in England shows that when athletes compete with a performance-approach mindset, they tend to perform above and beyond their expectations and perceived talent level. A performance-avoidance mindset, on the other hand, is often detrimental. A study published in the *Journal of Sport and Exercise Psychology* found that performance-avoidance goals led to worse functioning and evoked higher levels of angst, fear, and tightness when compared to performance-approach goals. Other studies show that while fear may work as a short-term motivator, it is a poor long-term one, leading to increased stress and burnout. Though these studies focused on athletes, I've observed the same pattern in the executives, entrepreneurs, and physicians whom I coach. When someone is deceiving themselves and not accepting of their reality, they become doubtful and insecure. When someone is honest with themselves and accepting of their reality, they gain a quiet and firm confidence.

The feminist and civil rights activist Audre Lorde embodied this kind of confidence. Lorde fought tirelessly against racism, sexism, and homophobia. She was not afraid to expose marginalization wherever she saw it—and sadly, she saw plenty. She was frequently attacked for these observations by a society that would rather have kept them swept under the rug. Even so, Lorde's writing offered a message of hope. She wrote with strength and love when it would have been easy to write with despair. "Nothing I accept about myself can be used to diminish me," she wrote in *Sister Outsider*, published in 1984. Her acceptance was not a vehicle to shrug off responsibility or effort. It was not about acquiescence or submission. Rather, Lorde's acceptance of herself and the situation of marginalized people granted her the opposite. It allowed her to stand tall and openhearted, to keep fighting the good fight, even when doing so meant going against all odds.

Another example of acceptance and performing from a place of love occurred during the early days of the COVID-19 pandemic, in the spring of 2020. Amid so much pain and suffering, with a health care system on the brink of being overwhelmed, Dr. Craig Smith, chair of the Department of Surgery at Columbia University Irving Medical Center, sent a daily update to faculty and staff about the hospital's priorities and response to the pandemic. Smith did not beat around the bush or view the situation with rose-tinted glasses. As you'll see in the following examples, his updates were accepting, honest, and often grim. But they were also full of love, and thus they supported playing to win during a critical juncture in modern history.

Nothing would give me greater pleasure than to apologize profusely in a few weeks for having overestimated the threat. . . . [But] the next month or two is a horror to imagine if we're underestimating the threat. So what can we do? Load the sled, check the traces, feed Balto, and mush on. Our cargo must reach Nome. Remember that our families, friends, and neighbors are scared, idle, out of work, and feel impotent. Anyone working in health care still enjoys the rapture of action. It's a privilege! We mush on. [March 20, 2020]

The New York Times features a full page of COVID-19 obituaries today. That will continue for a while. The first

Western expedition to traverse Africa, covering 7,000 miles over 3 years, lasted from 1874 to 1877. The dangers, privations, and assaults by disease were biblical. It started with 228 souls (including 36 women and 10 children). There were a few recruitments and desertions along the way, and 114 died—50% mortality. They managed to bring 108 souls home. It would have been 105, except that 3 children were born on the journey and survived to the end. Life finds a way. [March 29, 2020]

Dr. Smith's updates were widely circulated in hospitals across the country. His leadership helped the United States of America weather COVID-19's initial storm. Sadly, nonacceptance, denial, delusion, and unabashed heroic individualism by far too many other leaders led to an awful and tragic prolongment of the crisis.

Unfortunately, much in the current culture pushes people toward nonacceptance, toward performing from a place of avoidance and fear. This mindset generates cravings for specific and measurable results; for only by accomplishing these results, the thinking goes, are we worthy and whole. But this kind of craving is not associated with peak performance. It is, however, associated with anxiety, depression, burnout, and unethical behavior.* The stress and pressure of carrying this weight is miserable. It is only when you fully accept your current abilities and circumstances that you can perform from a place of freedom and play to win. After years of being tight, this can feel like having shackles removed.

One of my coaching clients, Blair, hated being asked, "Are you

---

*For more on this topic, see my previous book, *The Passion Paradox*, coauthored with Steve Magness.

ready?" before big meetings and presentations. It made him feel nervous, like he could always have done more and been better prepared. Blair and I worked together to understand that it didn't really matter—he was as ready as he was going to be. Accepting this was freedom. Blair came to embrace this, to feel it wholeheartedly and own it. Whenever others asked him if he was ready, or when he asked himself, he answered, "I'm as ready as I'm going to be." He became looser, more relaxed, and more open. He felt better, and he started performing better too. It's worth repeating that acceptance doesn't mean you can't change or improve. Over time, Blair did both. It just means that where you are today is where you are today; it's exactly where you need to be, and it's the key to getting where you want to go.

Sarah True spent months in therapy for her depression. Though as of this writing she is doing much better, you still can't tie a tidy bow on her story. She's a work in progress, and that's the point. "Acceptance is now a regular part of my life," she told me. "It's realizing that not every day is going to be perfect, and that's okay. It's about being humble. It's about constantly knowing where I am. I feel a deep freedom that comes from acknowledging my pain, my flaws, and my failures, and moving forward anyway," she says. Like all of us, True still has her struggles. But she feels stronger than she has in quite some time. Instead of denying her difficulties and pushing them under the rug, she accepts them as part of being human, even as part of being a world-class athlete. By fully accepting and confronting her reality, she's finally found more solid ground. True's next big challenge will be moving on from sport altogether as she approaches her retirement, something that happens at around forty for most endurance athletes. She's currently taking the prerequisite courses for graduate school, where she plans to pursue a degree in clinical psychology. "Isn't it remarkable how life can take us on these unexpected journeys?" she wrote me.

PRACTICE: CULTIVATE THE LENS OF A "WISE OBSERVER"

Rather than being so involved in whatever you are experiencing, it can be useful to step back and view it from afar. This helps create space between yourself and your situation so that you can accept it and view it more clearly. The lens of a wise observer can be cultivated via formal practice and also by developing tools you can call upon in everyday life. We'll cover both, starting with formal practice.

- Sit or lie down in a comfortable position. Set a timer for anywhere between five and twenty minutes. Close your eyes and focus on your breath. You can concentrate on the sensation of air moving in and out of your nostrils, the rising and falling of your belly, or any other place in your body where you feel it. Whenever your attention drifts away from your breath, simply notice it has drifted and bring it back to the breath, without berating yourself for getting distracted.

- Once you settle in, perhaps after a minute or two, though sometimes longer, imagine yourself as a life force that is separate from your thoughts, feelings, and circumstances. Imagine you are awareness itself—the canvas upon which all your thoughts, feelings, and circumstances arise, the container that holds everything. You can also imagine your awareness as a blue sky and anything that pops up as clouds floating by.

- Look through this lens of awareness to see your thoughts, feelings, and circumstances. It may start to feel as if you are watching a movie instead of being in it. When you get distracted or caught up in your experience, note it without judging yourself, and then return to concentrating on the sensation of your breath moving through your body. Once you've stabilized your awareness on your breath, go back to viewing your thoughts and feelings from afar.

- Let this awareness become a vessel to hold whatever it is you are grappling with. From this space, you can accept and see situations clearly, and thus make wiser decisions. The result of adopting this perspective is similar to the observer effect in quantum physics: when you change your relationship to what you are observing, the nature of what you are observing changes. In this case, challenges go from being permanent and insurmountable to impermanent and manageable.

- Keep practicing. You might notice that the stronger the thought, feeling, urge, or situation, the harder it is to maintain space between it and your awareness of it. But just a single degree of separation goes a long way. The more you practice, the more separation you'll be able to create, and the faster you'll be able to zoom out when you find yourself converging with a challenging experience.

The more you strengthen the perspective of a wise observer in formal practice, the more available it will be to you in daily life. The meditation teacher Michele McDonald developed a four-step method called RAIN that can help. When you find yourself resisting an experience or situation, pause for a moment and take a few breaths. As you do:

1. **R**ecognize what is happening.

2. **A**llow life to be just as it is.

3. **I**nvestigate your inner experience with kindness and curiosity.

4. **N**ote or practice non-identification, not fusing with what you are experiencing but rather viewing it from a larger perspective.

When you accept and evaluate your situation from a larger perspective, your ability to work with it in a skillful manner improves. Research shows this is true for everything from physical pain to emotional pain to social anxiety to making difficult decisions. The more space you can put between yourself and your experience, the better.

Another way to quickly tap into the lens of a wise observer is to use what researchers call *self-distancing*. Imagine that a friend is going through the same situation as you. How would you look at that friend? What advice would you give them? Studies conducted at the University of California, Berkeley, show that this method helps people accept their situations, see them more clearly, and take wiser actions, especially when the stakes are high. You can also imagine an older and wiser version of yourself—perhaps ten, twenty, or thirty years down the road. What advice would future you offer to present-day you? Can you follow that advice right now?

By creating space between yourself and your circumstances, you become more likely to accept them for what they are and in turn manage them more productively. You stop denying and resisting the hard stuff, while not completely fusing with it either. You begin to cultivate a sense of self that is deeper, more robust, and more grounded than your moment-to-moment, always-changing experience.

PRACTICE: CHOOSE SELF-COMPASSION OVER SELF-JUDGMENT

Accepting and seeing your situation clearly is hard, but doing something productive about it may be even harder. This is particularly true if you are not thrilled about what you find. Enter self-compassion. Self-compassion serves as the bridge between accepting what is happening and taking wise action. If your inner voice is overly judgmental and critical, you are likely to get stuck, or worse, go backward. You need to be kind to yourself. If you're not accustomed to this, it may sound soft and woo-woo, but I recommend you test your preconceived notions. Numerous studies show that individuals who react to challenging situations with self-compassion respond better than those who judge themselves harshly. The logic behind this is straightforward: if you judge yourself, you're liable to feel shame or guilt, and it is often this shame or guilt that keeps you trapped in your undesirable situation, preventing you from taking productive action. If, on the other hand, you can muster up kindness toward yourself, you gain the strength to move forward in a meaningful manner. The effects of self-compassion are true whether you are an eight-year-old who loves Disney fairy tales, a thirty-year-old professional football player, or a recently retired sixty-five-year-old.

Self-compassion doesn't come easily, especially for driven, type A people who are well-schooled at being hard on themselves. Think of it as an ongoing practice of giving yourself the benefit of the doubt. It's not that you want to forfeit self-discipline—it's that you want to marry self-discipline with self-compassion. When you do, you gain the ability to confront whatever is happening to you with greater strength and clarity. You also become more of a rock for other people to lean on. "What progress have I made?" wrote the Stoic philosopher Seneca, some two thousand years ago. "I am beginning to be my own friend. That is progress indeed. Such a person will never be alone, and you may be sure he is a friend of all."

- *Stop shoulding yourself.* Shift from an internal dialogue of *I shouldn't be in this situation* to *I wish I wasn't in this situation*; from *I should be going about this differently* to *I want to be going about this differently*. Language shapes reality, and these subtle shifts go a long way toward eliminating guilt, shame, and judgment and fostering self-compassion instead. When you catch yourself shoulding, try using another word and see what happens.

- *Treat yourself like a crying baby.* Anyone who has ever held a crying baby knows that yelling back at her only makes matters worse. There are two skillful ways to handle a crying baby: (1) hold it, cradle it, and show it love, or (2) let the baby cry it out. Intervening rarely works. The best you can do is to create a safe space for the baby to exhaust herself. We'd be wise to treat ourselves the same way.

  When we mess up, our inclination is to berate ourselves for failing and judge ourselves for falling behind. But that reaction almost always makes matters worse. Far more effective is to resist the urge to yell at ourselves, and show ourselves love instead. If that doesn't work, we must stop engaging in the situation and create space to do the equivalent of crying it out.

- *"This is what is happening right now. I'm doing the best I can."* It's one of my favorite mantras. When you confront a challenging situation and catch yourself firing second, third, and fourth arrows, simply stop and say in your head, or out loud softly, *This is what is happening right now. I'm doing the best I can.* Research shows that mantras like this are effective at defusing negative judgment and bringing you back into the present moment so that you can take productive action instead of resisting or ruminating. I used this particular mantra frequently as a new parent. When my infant would wake me up multiple times throughout the night, I'd catch myself spiraling into negative thoughts: *This is impossible. I'm not getting any sleep. I'm going to be miserable tomorrow. I'm never going to be able to fall back asleep. Maybe we made a mistake.* Replacing this negative self-talk with a firm but gentle, *This is what is happening right now. I'm doing the best I can,* nudged me back into the present moment so that I could accept the situation for what it was and take productive action, which often just meant a diaper change and falling back asleep. It wasn't my crying infant that kept me awake and unnerved. It was the story I was telling myself—the second, third, and fourth arrows. This tends to be the case for many challenges far beyond parenting.

PRACTICE: MOOD FOLLOWS ACTION

You cannot always control your circumstances, but you can control how you respond. Conventional wisdom holds that motivation leads to action: the better you feel and the more advantageous your situation, the more likely you'll be to take constructive action. While this can be true sometimes, more often than not it's the opposite. You don't need to feel good to get going. You need to get going and then you'll give yourself a chance at feeling good.

In addition to acceptance and commitment therapy, other evidence-based clinical approaches, such as cognitive behavioral therapy (CBT) and dialectical behavior therapy (DBT), place an immense focus on the behavior part of the equation. That's because it's hard, if not impossible, to control your thoughts, feelings, and external circumstances. Long-standing psychological research shows that the more you try to think or feel a certain way, the less likely you are to think or feel that way. You can't will yourself into a certain state of mind, and as discussed throughout this chapter, you can't will yourself into a new reality either. What you can control, however, is your behavior—that is, your actions. Taking actions that align with your values—regardless of how you are feeling—is often the catalyst for your situation to improve. In the scientific literature, this is called *behavioral activation*. In lay terms, and phrasing that I first heard from the podcast host Rich Roll, mood follows action.

The idea that mood follows action is enmeshed with the *C* and *T* components of ACT: *choosing* your response instead of impulsively reacting, and then *taking* productive action. It starts with knowing your core values. These are the foundational principles that represent your best self or the person you want to become. A few examples include authenticity, health, community, spirituality, presence, love, family, integrity, relationships, and creativity. It's worth spending some time to reflect on your own core values. I'd recommend trying to come up with between three and five.

Once you have identified your core values, they become guide rails for your actions. For example, if your core values include creativity, family, and authenticity, you could ask yourself: What would a creative person do in this situation? What would it look like to prioritize family? What would be the most authentic way to act? How you answer these questions guides your actions. At first it might feel like you are forcing yourself to get going. That's fine. Do it anyway. The research in behavioral activation and ACT shows that your situation will generally improve as a result.

Here's how the pieces come together:

- Accept where you are. This is often the hardest part of getting where you want to go.

- Use the lens of a wise observer to see your situation clearly without becoming fused to it. If your situation and your awareness of your situation begin to collapse on each other, pause, realize what is happening, take a few deep breaths, and zoom back out to gain space.

- If you start judging yourself or your situation harshly, or find yourself spiraling into rumination, try to practice self-compassion. *This is what is happening right now. I'm doing the best I can.*

- Once you feel like you've evaluated your situation from a place of acceptance and clarity, choose a response that aligns with your core values. You are making a conscious choice, responding instead of impulsively reacting. In many ways, this is the embodiment of wisdom.

- Act in accordance with your values, even if you don't feel like it. Mood follows action.

All of this is a lot easier said than done. But with repetition and practice this cycle gradually becomes more natural.

PRACTICE: RELAX AND WIN

When you find yourself tight, anxious, or insecure about an important endeavor in your life, pause and remember that you're as ready as you're going to be. Take a breath or two and imagine that nothing is wrong. What would that feel like? When I go through this exercise with my coaching clients they tend to report that their chest opens, their respiration slows, and their shoulders drop. Now ask yourself: Which physical state is more conducive to peak performance? Anxious and tight or relaxed and open? Unanimously, my clients tell me they prefer the latter.

Judson Brewer, a Brown University neuroscientist and author of *Unwinding Anxiety*, found that when we shift from worrying about and trying to control a situation to accepting and being with it, activity in the posterior cingulate cortex (PCC) decreases. The PCC is a brain region associated with self-referential thinking, or getting caught up in one's experience. The more PCC activity, the less likely we are to enter a high-performance flow state. "In a sense, if we try to control a situation (or our lives) we have to work hard at *doing* something to get the results we want," Brewer writes. "In contrast, we can relax into an attitude that is more like a dance with the object, simply *being* with it as the situation unfolds, no striving or struggling necessary, as we get out of our own way."

As Bud Winter, widely regarded as one of the greatest track and field coaches, was known for saying, "Relax and win." Intuitively, this makes sense. Worrying about a situation or denying it altogether does not change it, but it does waste a lot of energy. What is happening right now is what is happening right now. You might as well accept it, because you're as ready as you're going to be.

FINAL THOUGHTS ON ACCEPTANCE

Acceptance is about being with your reality, whatever it may be. By doing so, you lessen the distress caused by wanting things to be different and judging yourself when they are not. You rid yourself of the gap between your expectations and your experience, and you eliminate the second, third, and fourth arrows. Only once you've accepted your reality will you find peace, strength, and stability, or at least an understanding of the actions you might take to attain these states. Acceptance is not about doing nothing. Rather, it is about reckoning with what is in front of you so you can encounter it in a skillful manner. Acceptance is necessary to experience contentment and happiness in the here and now, and it is the first step toward making progress in the future. It can be applied to every level of life. Whatever it is you are working toward—big or small, micro or macro—acceptance is an essential and ongoing practice. If you accept your reality you'll feel more firmly grounded in it. You'll be where you are, and you'll have a much better chance of getting where you want to go.

3

BE PRESENT SO YOU CAN OWN YOUR ATTENTION AND ENERGY

With their celebration of heroic individualism—of more, more, more; of enthusiastic one-upmanship—Western societies place optimization on a pedestal. We marvel at artificial intelligence, laud productivity, and measure everything, from the number of steps we take to the number of hours we sleep. As you'll see in the data presented throughout this chapter, we seek to do more and more, faster and faster, in an effort to get better and better. This is a rational desire. Except there's one major problem. Contrary to what heroic individualism would have you believe, we aren't machines. Computers and robots can dual-process. They do not experience fatigue. Nor do they have rich emotional lives that depend on the quality of their attention. We humans are different. When we strive to be everywhere and do everything, we tend to feel like we're not fully experiencing anything. If we're not careful and protective of our attention, it can seem like we're losing control of our lives, bouncing from one distraction to the next. This conundrum is not novel. Thousands of years ago, the Stoic philosopher Seneca warned against getting caught in a cycle of "busy idleness," or as he said, "all this dashing about that a great many people indulge in . . . always giving the impression of being busy [while not really doing anything at all]."

If being overly busy and scattered is a timeless problem, there is reason to believe it is also a particularly timely one. We live amid an ethos that emphasizes speed, quantity, and always doing something; technology that allows and encourages us to be online at all times; and an economy that is increasingly based on products and services that have an incentive to win over and control our attention.

A common example of heroic individualism's futile efforts to get more done faster at the expense of deep attention is multitasking—both physical and psychological. Contrary to what most people believe, studies show that when we multitask we are not doing or thinking about two things at once. Rather, our brains are constantly switching between tasks or dividing and conquering, allotting only a portion of our cognitive capacity to one task at a time. Researchers at the University of Michigan found that though we think we're getting twice as much done when we multitask, we're actually getting only about half as much done, and with a lower level of quality and enjoyment. A study conducted by King's College London found that persistent interruptions, such as the kind caused by multitasking, led to a ten-point drop in IQ. This is twice the decrease one experiences after using cannabis and on par with the decrease you'd expect from having stayed up all night. Multitasking is great, we tell ourselves. It's being überproductive, optimizing, getting so much done! But this story is an illusion.

It's not just performance that suffers when our attention is scattered, but emotional well-being too. Constant interruptions and nonstop busyness exact a severe toll on mental health. Researchers from Harvard found that when people are fully present for their activities, they are much happier and more fulfilled than when they're thinking about something else. The more scattered people are, the more likely they are to feel angst and discontent. "A wandering mind," the researchers write, "is an unhappy mind." This is likely one of the reasons that video chats on computers quickly become tedious and exhausting—what some have coined *Zoom fatigue*—when we've got other programs up and running at the same time (or when we're constantly moving away from the conversation to check email, news, or social media).

What's scary is how much of the average person's life is spent under fragmented attention. It is increasingly becoming our default way of operating. Studies have found that, on average, people spend 47 percent of their waking hours thinking about something other than what is in front of them. We've been conditioned to believe that if we aren't constantly scheming and strategizing, taking inventory of the past, or thinking ahead to the future, we'll miss out on something and fall behind. But perhaps the opposite is true. If we're constantly scheming and strategizing, always looking back or thinking ahead, we'll miss out on everything.

The second principle of groundedness is *presence*. It is about being fully here for what is in front of you. Presence is a concentrated quality of mind that lends itself to strength and stability. If you deliberately practice presence, it can drastically improve your life, both personal and professional. But before we delve deeper into its benefits, we must first spend a bit more time exploring its barriers. Unfortunately, presence is increasingly harder to come by. Only once we understand why this is the case can we begin to overcome it.

ADDICTED TO DISTRACTION

More than anything else, digital devices have made it possible for us to be in a constant state of distraction. Research from the United Kingdom's telecom regulator shows that the average person checks their phone every twelve minutes—and this doesn't include instances when someone is thinking about checking their phone but does not. Other research shows that 71 percent of people never turn their phone off and 40 percent look at their phone within five minutes of waking up, and that's apart from checking the alarm clock. And it's not just when we are physically glancing at our devices that our attention suffers. That's because all this checking habituates us to distraction. In essence, we are training our brains to be in a constant state of hyper-alertness, always thinking about what could be happening somewhere else and feeling the urge to check in and see. While this kind of behavior was advantageous during earlier phases of our species' evolution—it helped us avoid predators and find prey in times of scarcity, for example—it's not a great formula for living a happy, healthy, fulfilled life in the twenty-first century.

Stuart McMillan has spent the past twenty years of his life immersed in high-performance cultures, having coached more than thirty-five Olympic medalists in track and field. Stu (as I know him) has become a good friend. When we discuss the biggest challenges he's facing today, it's not just hamstring injuries or performance anxiety. It's also digital distraction. "For you and me, phones are a distraction from life," he says. "For some of the athletes I coach, life is a distraction from phones—even at the freakin' Olympics."

According to Adam Alter, author of the book *Irresistible* and a behavioral scientist who studies digital devices at New York University, a big reason that all of us, including McMillan's athletes, can't put down our phones or log off our email is because we've come to associate nonstop notifications with validating our importance in the world. Each and every notification we get—the Likes, retweets, comments, emails, texts—sends the message, however superficial, that we exist and matter. And that's a pretty significant reward to pursue. Picking up and refreshing our digital devices is like playing an existential slot machine. No wonder so many of us get hooked.

Beyond our desire to feel relevant, the attention-economy merchants also try to take advantage of our innate neural systems. Everything about the apps we check on our phones—the internet, news feeds, and social media, from the dramatic headlines to the riveting background music to the colors on the screen (lots of red, which experts agree is one of, if not the most, emotionally charged colors)—is engineered to prey on our hardwired impulses to pay attention to what *seems* important and exciting. The manner in which the news is presented, be it on television, websites, or the apps on our phones, often triggers the release of dopamine, a powerful neurochemical that tags experiences as meaningful and makes us want to seek them over and over again. In his book *Riveted*, Jim Davies, a professor of cognitive science at Carleton

University in Ontario, writes, "high dopamine makes everything look significant. . . . The news needs a fear to monger, regardless of how important it is. It deemphasizes the routine and constant, and brings irregularities to our attention."

In 1951, writing in *The Wisdom of Insecurity*, the philosopher Alan Watts lamented that "this dope that we call our high standard of living, a violent and complex stimulation of the senses, makes you progressively less sensitive and thus in need of yet more violent stimulation. We crave distraction—a panorama of sights, sounds, thrills, and titillations into which as much as possible must be crowded in the shortest period of time." The addiction is not new. It's just that today's dope is exponentially more accessible and powerful.

LESS CANDY, MORE NOURISHMENT— A BETTER WAY TO OPTIMIZE

All the notifications, news, and other distractions that are ubiquitous in today's society are like candy. We crave it and it tastes good while we are eating it, but it's empty calories, never filling us up, providing no real nourishment. If anything, it tends to make us feel gross, especially when we consume it in large quantities. No retweet, Like, nine p.m. message from the boss, Instagram post, or "breaking" news story is more meaningful or satisfying than being present for the people and pursuits we care about most.

In *The Art of Living*, Zen master Thich Nhat Hanh writes, "It has become a habit to reach for the phone or computer and immerse ourselves in another world. We do it to survive. But we want to do more than just survive. We want to live." I tend to agree. We are optimizing for all the wrong things: Busyness. Nonstop information. Digital relevance. It is easy to convince ourselves that we are getting so much done when in fact we are hardly getting anything done, at least not of real value. It is not surprising that unrelenting distraction leaves people feeling unfulfilled. You don't get full eating loads of candy. What you get is an ephemeral high followed by sickness and regret.

Optimization in and of itself is not a bad thing. But we are going about it all wrong. According to Merriam-Webster's dictionary, the definition of *optimize* is "to make as perfect, effective, or functional as possible." *Optimize* is derived from the Latin *optimus*, which simply means "best." If the goal is to optimize, we shouldn't be focused on doing more for the sake of doing more. Rather, we should be focused on being fully present for the pursuits and people that matter most to us. As you'll soon see, when we optimize in this way, we feel our best, and we perform our best, too. Doing stuff is only valuable if the stuff we are doing is valuable.

Ed Batista is a lecturer at the prestigious Stanford Graduate School of Business (GSB) and a counselor to numerous top executives in Silicon Valley. His course, the Art of Self-Coaching, is one of the most popular in the GSB, known for its focus on students' humanity, not just their management skills. With both his students and clients, and certainly in his own life, Batista emphasizes the importance of presence and owning one's attention. For him, this starts with honestly evaluating trade-offs. "We often think about the potential value of what we're adding to our plates, but we rarely consider at what cost," he says. In other words, it is important to remember that whenever you say yes to something you are saying no to something else.

Batista's mindset doesn't only apply to meetings or projects. It's also about the small decisions you make throughout the day. Every time you check your phone you sacrifice the potential for a creative thought that could have filled that space. Every time you shift out of focus to respond to an email, you do so at the expense of progress in an endeavor that might matter. Every time you get caught up in thinking about something that happened in the past or might happen in the future, you lose the ability to connect intimately to the person or work in front of you. "Attention is a finite resource," Batista says. "And attention vampires are lurking everywhere, literally sucking the life out of us."

Batista is a big proponent of deliberately designing his surroundings in a way that is conducive to protecting his attention. "Setting up the right environment externally makes it much easier internally, in my head," he says. This may mean leaving his phone turned off and in another room, or his internet browser and email client closed. Studies show that merely having these potential distractions in sight reduces the quality of our presence, even if we aren't using them. Researchers speculate this occurs for two reasons: (1) it takes a fair amount of mental energy to resist checking these devices, and (2) they summon everything else that is happening in the world, the thought of which is a massive distraction in and of itself. Even if your phone is facedown and on silent, it is difficult not to think about what is happening on the other side. If your phone is within your line of sight, it is probably contributing to the deterioration of your presence and attention.*

Establishing firm boundaries is another concept that Batista teaches and embodies. He has no problem declining to engage with people and projects that don't interest him or that would leave him feeling scattered and rushed. "If we find ourselves in situations where we can't manage our attention, then it's also worth asking, *What am I doing here?*" he says. "I'm not suggesting we should always be automatically entranced with what is in front of us. But if we're always bored and distracted, maybe that's a sign we shouldn't be spending our time, attention, and energy on that particular person or pursuit."

Here, Batista brings to mind the Stoic philosopher Seneca and his master work, *On the Shortness of Life*, written around AD 49. "It is not that we have a short time to live," Seneca writes. "It is that we waste a lot of it. . . . People are frugal in guarding their personal property, but as soon as it comes to squandering time they are most wasteful of the one thing in which it is right to be stingy." Seneca and the Stoics taught that life is actually quite long if we know how to live it. When we protect our time, energy, and attention and direct it wisely—when we are present for meaningful people, places, and pursuits—our entire experience of being alive improves dramatically.

---

*For more on this topic, see my book *Peak Performance*, coauthored with Steve Magness.

TOUCHING BLISS—WHEN CUTTING-EDGE SCIENCE MEETS ANCIENT WISDOM

When you are fully present for what is in front of you, you become more likely to enter *flow*, a state in which you are completely absorbed in an activity—be it running, lovemaking, painting, writing code, solving math proofs, engaging in good conversation, meditating, surfing, you name it. In flow, your perceptions of time and space are altered. You enter what is colloquially referred to as "the zone." Decades of psychological research show that people perform best and feel best when they enter this state. A critical precondition for flow is the elimination of distractions so that you can focus completely on whatever it is you are doing.

Another common feature of flow is the shedding of self-consciousness. It is as if you become one with your experience. The delineation between subject and object, between you and your activity, melts away. Though only over the past few decades have scientists documented this defining element of flow, the world's major wisdom traditions have been pointing toward it for millennia. Consider the following: In Buddhism, the goal of the spiritual path, if there is one, is Nirvana, or the dissolution of self in connection with something larger, with an ever-expanding spaciousness and timelessness. Taoism's central concept, the Way, is described as a non-dual experience, the merging of subject and object—often represented by yin and yang. The Stoics wrote that lasting satisfaction arises when one's attention is fully absorbed in their work or conversation. In ancient Greece, a primary moral virtue was *arête*, or excellence via the application of complete presence in one's craft. The Greeks believed that through arête someone expresses their full potential. They get the most out of themselves, and in doing so, they share their unique talents with their community. Though these traditions evolved in different parts of the world, their shared message is clear. We are at our best when we are fully absorbed in the present moment.

In a study out of Harvard, psychologists Matthew Killingsworth and Daniel Gilbert wanted to better understand the link between someone's presence and their emotional state. They developed an iPhone app (the irony of this is not lost on me) that contacted more than 2,250 volunteers at random intervals to ask how happy they were, what they were currently doing, and whether they had been concentrating on their current activity or thinking about the past or future. Killingsworth and Gilbert found that the quality of one's presence determined the quality of their life. "How often our minds leave the present and where they tend to go is a better predictor of our happiness than the activities in which we are engaged," says Killingsworth. The more present we are, the better. The parallels between their findings and the teachings of ancient wisdom traditions were not lost on Killingsworth and Gilbert. "Many philosophical and religious traditions teach that happiness is to be found by living in the moment," they write in the journal *Science*. The results of their study, they conclude, prove these ancient teachings are right.

In a separate study, also out of Harvard, researchers have been tracking the physical and emotional well-being of more than seven hundred people who grew up in Boston during the 1930s and 1940s. It is one of the longest and most comprehensive studies of its kind, closely following subjects from their late teens and early twenties all the way into their eighties and nineties. In this way, the Harvard Study of Adult Development is well positioned to answer questions about what it means to live a good, fulfilling life. Many of the findings are what you'd expect: don't drink too much, don't smoke, exercise often, eat a nutritious diet, maintain a healthy body weight, and keep learning. But according to George Vaillant, a psychiatrist and clinical therapist who directed the study for more than three decades, the most important component to a good and long life is love. "The 75 years and 20 million dollars spent on the Grant Study points to a straightforward five-word conclusion," Vaillant writes. "Happiness equals love—full stop."

What is love—be it for a person, for a pursuit, or for life itself—if not presence, if not resounding attention and caring? When we are fully present, we enter a sacred space, one where the philosopher and aikido master George Leonard said "God lives." Perhaps this space is where love lives, too. Who knows, maybe God, love, Nirvana, the Way, arête, and flow are all one and the same.

LIFE IS NOW

In 2008, when Mike Posner was a twenty-year-old undergraduate student at Duke University, he wrote a song called "Cooler Than Me" in his dorm room. It was a unique track, a mash-up of pop and electronica before this sort of mix was common. Radio stations in his hometown of Detroit loved the song. I know this because I was living just outside the city shortly after "Cooler Than Me" dropped, and for a few solid months, the song's chorus was the backdrop to my every car ride, barbershop visit, gym session, and café experience. It wasn't long before the song spread beyond Detroit, and in May 2010, it reached number two on the Billboard Hot 100. Posner—who as a child worried his parents because, in his own words, he "didn't talk to nobody, just made beats"—had arrived. In 2016, Posner released his second album, *At Night, Alone,* which included the massive hit "I Took a Pill in Ibiza," a reflection on the highs, lows, and more than occasional emptiness of stardom. Posner assumed that signing a record deal and becoming famous would make him happy, but he was mistaken. The money, sex, drugs, and massive shows weren't all they were cracked up to be.

It wasn't until 2019 that Posner released his next album, *A Real Good Kid.* A lot had happened in the previous four years. His good friend Tim Bergling, the iconic electronic dance music artist known by his stage name, Avicii, died by suicide. Posner broke up with his girlfriend. And his dad, his best friend in the world, passed away at age seventy-three due to fast-progressing brain cancer. While Posner's past albums tended toward the jovial and upbeat, *A Real Good Kid* confronted his recent and dark past. He says the creation of this album helped him process his grief. The entire album is vulnerable and raw. There are parts when Posner is unmistakably distraught, yelling and crying. I remember being blown away the first time I listened to the album. Posner's presence—his pain, suffering, questioning, healing, joy, all of it—ran through my headphones and into my heart. I was in George Leonard's sacred space with him. This is not by accident. *A Real Good Kid* opens with a short introduction in which Posner implores the listener: "The album is forty minutes long and is meant to be listened to in one sitting, straight through. It is meant to be listened to without texting, without emailing, without outside distraction of any sort. If at this time you are unable to devote forty minutes of undivided attention, I politely ask you turn this off and return at a later time."

When I spoke with Posner about a year after *A Real Good Kid* was released, he told me that he'd felt down when the album first came out. He dreaded the endless self-promotion, the highs and lows of touring, and the superficial facade of connection that accompanies playing the role of a pop star. Loss was still at the forefront of his mind. He had gained a visceral appreciation that he, too, was going to die. "So I said fuck it," he told me. "I want to walk across America. It's something I've always dreamed of doing and I am not going to wait. I don't know how long I am going to be here for. So I am going to do it now." His record label wasn't thrilled, but Posner didn't care. He wasn't going on tour. He wasn't doing all the late-night shows. He was walking across the country, escaping all the noise in hopes of finding some signal, yearning to quench his thirst for lasting fulfillment.

On April 15, 2019, Mike Posner set out from Asbury Park, New Jersey, to walk across the United States of America. Six months later, on Friday, October 18, he finished in Venice Beach, California. The 2,851-mile trek was beyond anything Posner could have imagined. In eastern Colorado, he got bit on the ankle by a rattlesnake and almost died. He was airlifted to a hospital, where he spent five days in the intensive care unit followed by weeks of rehab. But Posner was determined. Once he regained the strength to walk, he went back to the location where he'd been bitten and started walking again. But even more so than the physical challenges, he told me it was the emotional journey that had the most profound impact on him. "I went to places I didn't know existed," he said. "I learned how to be present for the highs and lows and to get through them, even to stay strong and solid."

In some of the communities he walked through, Posner played small acoustic pop-up shows. He told me that these shows reminded him of the things he loved most about making music: the deep connection and felt presence, both with his songs and with his audience. "The more I feel loved by my community the less I care about all the distractions, all the noise, the retweets, the Likes, the comments. . . . It just doesn't matter," he says. "Life slowed down. For the first time in a long time I felt grounded. It was beautiful." Posner realized that how he had been thinking about happiness and fulfillment was misguided. "I used to think there was an end zone or a goalpost that I'd arrive at. But that's not true. There is no end zone. It's a day-to-day decision. How do I want to show up? Where do I want to direct my energy and attention? What do I want to be present for? Answering those questions with integrity—that's how you find happiness."

Shortly after finishing the walk, Posner posted a video on YouTube. It's set to a song of his, "Live Before I Die." In the middle of the video, in big, bold, all-cap letters, "LIFE IS NOW" appears on the screen. Perhaps more than anything, this is what Posner's walk taught him, and can help teach all of us. To be grounded is to be here—to really be *here*—for our lives right now. Yes, Posner's walk was dramatic. But you can go on a similar journey in parenting, creativity, art, sports, or any other pursuit. If you pay close attention to how you are paying attention, you will viscerally experience the power of grounding yourself and losing yourself—and realize those seeming opposites are actually one and the same. People often think about the number of years in their lives. But perhaps more important is the amount of life, the amount of presence, in those years.

FORGET ABOUT PRODUCTIVITY—THINK ABOUT *PRODUCTIVE* ACTIVITY INSTEAD

When he was setting out on his walk Posner repeatedly stated, "I'm not walking to show people who I am. I'm walking to find out who I'll become." In this sentiment lies a crucial paradox of presence. When you are fully present you not only shape your experience of the now, but you also shape your future.

Someone who understood this well was Erich Fromm, a German Jew who fled the Nazi regime and moved to the United States in 1933. He was a polymath: a brilliant psychologist, sociologist, and humanistic philosopher. In 1976, Fromm wrote a book titled *To Have or to Be?* In it, he coined the term *productive activity*: when one's activity is "a manifestation of their powers; when the person, their activity, and the result of their activity are one." If this sounds familiar, that's because it is. Fromm's productive activity is strikingly similar to what modern scientists call flow, what Buddhism calls Nirvana, what Taoism calls the Way, and what the ancient Greeks called arête.

Fromm believed that productive activity is generative of not only one's best work but also one's best life. In his theory, the quality of your productive activity shapes what you do today, and what you do today shapes who you'll be tomorrow. His productive activity relies on a foundation of what he called *concentration* and *supreme concern*—or what we've been calling *presence*. According to Fromm, in order to do your best work and become your best self, you need to cultivate presence and then direct that presence toward meaningful, productive activities. His concept of productive activity is very different from modern ways of thinking about productivity. Whereas the latter tends to be frenetic and scattered, the former is intentional and thoughtful. Productive activity has nothing to do with being swept away by the inertia of busyness. It is not about quantity, either. Rather, it is a deliberate choice of where and how to direct one's attention.

The significance of this choice cannot be overstated. Research increasingly shows that what is important doesn't necessarily get our attention, but what gets our attention becomes important. This mirrors a concept in ancient Buddhist psychology that is often referred to as *selective watering*. In short, the mind contains a diverse variety of seeds: joy, integrity, anger, jealousy, greed, love, delusion, creativity, and so on. Buddhist psychology taught that we should think of ourselves as gardeners and our presence and attention as nourishment for the seeds. The seeds that we water are the seeds that grow. The seeds that grow shape the kind of person we become. In other words, the quality of our presence—its intensity and where we choose to channel it—determines the quality of our lives.

More than two thousand years after these Buddhist teachings were first recorded, the writer David Foster Wallace, in his popular "This Is Water" commencement address at Kenyon College in Ohio in 2005, said, "Learning how to think really means being conscious and aware enough to choose what you pay attention to and to choose how you construct meaning from experience. Because if you cannot exercise this kind of choice in adult life, you will be totally hosed." Foster Wallace is right.

Hopefully by now the perils of distraction and the benefits of presence are clear. Understanding these is one thing, but putting them into practice is another. Presence is not automatic. Just because you can intellectually grasp it doesn't mean you'll embody it. You need to train it like any other muscle. Nearly all my executive coaching clients struggle with distraction and nonstop busyness. At times I do, too. I think just about everyone does. We all want to be more present. We all understand the advantages of being more present. And yet we all still struggle with how to actually *be* more present. What follows are a few concrete practices to help. It's not easy to give up a life of distraction for a life of presence. But you can make incremental progress. The effort is worth it.

PRACTICE: STEP OUT OF THE DISTRACTION CANDY STORE

It is hard to choose brown rice and vegetables if you are constantly surrounded by peanut M&M's. Presence, flow, and productive activity become more accessible when you remove the candy, the distractions. Many of the digital devices that prey on your attention are designed by highly skilled engineers and experts in behavioral addiction. Their goal is to get you hooked, and they are proficient at it. Trying to resist the distractions caused by these devices is generally a losing proposition. Thus, it can be helpful to think of willpower as something that materializes not in the moment you want to be present, but upstream of it. Perhaps the most famous scene in Homer's epic *Odyssey* is when Ulysses, the story's main protagonist, wants to hear the Sirens' song, knowing that doing so would render him incapable of rational thought. Its irresistible beauty would distract him from his mission and tempt him to join enemy forces. So Ulysses puts wax in the ears of his crew so they can't hear, and then instructs them to tie him to the mast of the ship and not release him under any circumstance. Now he will be able to hear the song without becoming a slave to it. In philosophy circles, this is known as the Ulysses pact. Its lesson is that when we are faced with great temptation, willpower alone is almost never enough.

Getting upstream of tempting distractions is a two-step process: identify times when you want to engage in deep-focus work or fully present play and connection, and then eliminate distractions prior to those times.

- Block off periods on your calendar for full presence, or make them part of your regular routine. Knowing what you are going to do in these blocks ahead of time is key. Without this step of planning and intentionality, distraction too easily encroaches upon presence.

- Have a plan in place for where you'll store your digital devices and how you'll eliminate other distractions.

Remember that even the mere sight of some digital devices, like phones or computers, can interfere with your ability to be present. Turning them off may not be enough. Out of sight *really is* out of mind. I've had clients who leave their phones and computers in their basements, or who leave their offices to go to cafés without wireless connections. This step is especially important if you are prone to checking your email, Likes, retweets, or comments on social media. Remember, swiping for these notifications is akin to playing an existential slot machine. It is hard to pay attention to anything but gambling when you are in a casino.

- Don't be surprised if you feel worse before you feel better. If you are accustomed to being tethered to your digital devices all the time, then leaving them behind may be stressful. Start with small chunks of distraction-free time, even twenty minutes, and gradually increase the duration. Psychologists call this process *exposure and response prevention*, or ERP. This treatment is the gold standard for anxiety. You expose yourself to the thing that makes you anxious and then you prevent the response that would otherwise make the anxiety go away. In this case, the exposure is being fully present without checking your device or worrying about the past or future, and the response you are preventing is checking your phone or getting caught up in rumination.

- With ERP, feelings of restlessness and angst may increase at first, but they improve over time. Just knowing this helps, particularly if you have a hard time at the outset. Stick with the practice. After a few weeks your brain will relearn that the world doesn't end when you leave your phone behind and that you need not constantly worry about the past or future. As a consequence, you'll be better able to settle into the present moment without becoming distracted. You'll accomplish more meaningful work, feel increasingly stable, and experience more fulfillment and satisfaction.

- One last point to note: be sure to give yourself a few minutes to groove into deep focus and presence. Like candy, distractions are almost always more appealing in the moment. It takes a little while to feel good about eating brown rice instead. Nine out of ten times when I sat down to work on this book it would have been much easier to tweet, respond to emails, or browse news and politics websites. But after a few minutes of sinking into a rhythm, I was always glad to be writing and not doing that other stuff.

You might think that if some presence is good then more must be better, so why not try to avoid distractions throughout the entire day? While this is a noble aim, for many of us, me included, it is unrealistic. What ends up happening is that we cave in to the temptation for novelty and distraction and then berate ourselves for doing so. I suggest a different approach with my coaching clients. I have them set aside blocks of time for undistracted work and intimate connection and then, during the rest of the day, whatever happens, happens. If they check their email a gazillion times, that's fine, so long as they don't check it during their set-aside blocks for presence. This way, instead of constantly failing or trying to avoid a negative outcome (not getting distracted), they are patterning success and accomplishing a positive outcome (the feeling of being fully present). Over time, the more you experience full presence, the less enticing distractions become. This process moves you toward an entire life of presence.

I once had a coaching client named Tim, a highly successful salesperson who was accustomed to being online always. Though he didn't like how this made him feel, he could hardly imagine another way of existing. We started by committing to two thirty-minute blocks of deep-focus work throughout the day, and in the evening, turning off his phone and storing it in a drawer at eight p.m. After four months of us working together, Tim was doing three ninety-minute blocks of deep-focus work on most days and putting his phone away by six thirty p.m. When I asked him about his transformation, he said it was fairly simple: he kept achieving little victories. He gradually realized that the more present he was, the better he performed and the better he felt. "The first week or two were hard. I definitely felt nervous that I was falling behind and had the subsequent urge to pull up my email. But I stuck with it." Eventually, he learned to actually enjoy eating brown rice and vegetables more than peanut M&M's. "I realized that I had been fooling myself; most emails and messages do not require an immediate response. Most things can wait a few hours." As Tim reclaimed his attention and capacity for presence, he reclaimed hours and hours of his life. He spent more time on the activities and people that mattered to him and less time on the ephemeral and shallow. He began to feel like he was on more solid ground. Tim's story represents an important lesson. The best way to attain a life without distraction is to start small and gradually build over time. Begin with minutes, progress to hours, and eventually you'll get to days.

PRACTICE: SURF WAVES OF DISTRACTION

You won't always be able to tie yourself to the mast (as Ulysses did) or remove all distractions. And it's not like you can control your own thoughts, feelings, and urges—which often interrupt focus. But what you can do is feel the temptation to turn toward distraction or to get caught up in thinking about something else and *not* act on it. "Each time you ride a wave of craving without giving in," says Brown University neuroscientist Judson Brewer, "you stop reinforcing the habit." In essence, you learn how to feel an urge to eat candy without needing to eat it. "These waves are like inverted U's—you can feel them rise, crest, then fall," Brewer says. Your work is to surf the waves.

As you practice surfing waves of distraction, there will be moments in which you succumb. You'll check your phone. Dive into the rabbit hole of email or social media. Get caught up in thinking about the past or worrying about the future. That's fine. Just pay close attention to how you feel during and after this happens. Odds are you'll feel good for a bit, but then, as with eating too many chocolates, you may begin to feel lousy. The more deeply you feel the dissatisfaction that comes with a day spent in distraction, or even briefly interrupting moments of full presence, the easier it becomes to ride the next wave of distraction without getting swallowed by it. In essence, you are training your brain to identify distractions as meaningless noise—not meaningful signals.

The flip side is also true: it is helpful to feel presence deeply. This sounds obvious, but as you transition to being more present, you might find yourself emerging from flow states and back into the world of distraction so swiftly that you never appreciate how good it felt to be in the zone. Take a few moments after a fully present period to reflect on your experience. An easy way to do this, one that I often use with my coaching clients, is by journaling. Spend a minute or two jotting down a few words to describe your fully present experience. The more you reflect on and internalize how it feels to be fully present, the less likely you'll be to give in to distractions. You'll realize in a visceral way that the hollow, fleeting, candy-like rewards you get from distractions—from a day checking your emails, Likes, comments, and retweets—pale in comparison to the far more satiating gift of being fully present for the meaningful people and projects in your life.

PRACTICE: DEVELOP MINDFULNESS

When you envision meditation you might see someone sitting cross-legged with their eyes closed in a blissed-out state. This is how the practice is often portrayed in the media, at least in the West. But this portrayal generates a big misconception: that the primary purpose of meditation is to help you relax. This couldn't be further from the truth. Mindfulness, the variety of meditation we'll be discussing here, develops wisdom, compassion, and the presence to be fully in your life.

Every time you sit in silence and attempt to focus on your breath, many thoughts, feelings, and urges—often unpleasant ones—will arise. The practice of mindfulness involves not engaging in the thoughts, feelings, and urges and returning to your breath instead. "Your work is simply seeing and letting go, seeing and letting go, sometimes ruthlessly and relentlessly if need be . . . Just seeing and letting go, seeing and letting be," writes the meditation teacher Jon Kabat-Zinn.

Mindfulness teaches you to let an itch, be it a physical or meta-phorical one, be there without scratching it. You see and feel it, smile at it, and refocus on the breath. What you'll find is that left unscratched, most itches resolve on their own. If you practice mindfulness regularly, many of the proverbial itches in your life lose their power over you, allowing you to more seamlessly direct your attention where you want. You gain the ability to notice distractions—both external and internal—and then nonjudgmen-tally redirect your attention back to what is important, instead of reacting to everything that comes your way. This doesn't happen overnight. You need to practice regularly.

"Deep-seated, habitual thought patterns require constant mind-fulness repeatedly applied over whatever time period it takes to break their hold," writes the monk Bhante Gunaratana. "Distrac-tions are really paper tigers. They have no power of their own. They need to be fed constantly, or else they die." The latest sci-ence agrees. Studies show that attention is like a muscle. Paying attention now strengthens your ability to pay attention in the future. Likewise, getting caught up in distraction now makes it more likely you'll do so in the future.

You can practice mindfulness both formally and informally.

- *During formal practice,* set a timer for between three and forty-five minutes and sit or lie down in a comfortable position. Start small and increase the duration over time. It's better to begin with a few minutes of formal practice per day and stay consistent than to shoot for the moon and constantly fall short. Next, direct your attention to the sensation of your breath wherever you feel it most strongly, be it the nose, chest, or abdomen. When your attention drifts from your breath toward thoughts, feelings, or urges, simply note without judgment that it has drifted, and then bring your attention back to the breath. If you start judging yourself for being distracted, try not to judge yourself for judging yourself! Just pay attention to what is happening, noticing it all unfold, not clinging to anything. That's all there is to it. The practice is as simple and as hard as that. If you are struggling with meditation, that's not a bad thing. It's a sign that you are improving. Simply noticing how hard it can be to focus on your breath without becoming distracted is an important and valuable insight in and of itself. And you gain self-compassion from realizing, up close and personal, how often we habitually judge ourselves and how little we gain from it. Eventually, you may even learn to laugh at all this internal chatter.

- *Informally, throughout the day, the practice of mindfulness* is noticing when your attention drifts from whatever or whomever you want to be present for, and then gently nudging it back.

In both informal and formal practice the goal is not to never be distracted. Even lifetime monks get distracted. The goal is to more quickly notice when you are distracted without beating yourself up about it, so that you can redirect your attention to where you want it. The result is that you end up owning more of your attention, and thus owning more of your life.

A formal mindfulness meditation practice can also be combined with adopting the lens of a wise observer, from chapter 2. You can work on your presence skills for the first few minutes by repeatedly returning to the breath, and then zoom out and adopt a larger perspective, that of a wise observer, afterward. You could also do this in the other direction.

PRACTICE: MAKE A NOT-TO-DO LIST

Though the exact date is unknown, sometime in the 1200s the Chinese Zen master Wumen Huikai wrote, "If your mind isn't clouded by unnecessary things, this is the best season of your life."

I had Huikai's insight in mind in 2019 when I began working with a coaching client named Michelle. Michelle is a senior manager at a large organization. She deeply understands the value of presence, but was struggling to practice it since getting promoted to a new role with more direct reports and projects. As a result,

Michelle was feeling like she had little to no control over her day. Compounded over time, this scattered feeling was leading her down an increasingly steep slope toward burnout. She wasn't spending her time, energy, and attention on the activities she wanted, which was causing her significant frustration, resentment, and anger. Her colleagues were noticing, and her partner was noticing, too. Michelle was not watering the seeds in her life that she wanted to be watering, and it was showing.

I asked her to tell me everything she dreads about her job—all the stuff with little to no value—that was throwing her off. She made a long list. Then I asked her why she doesn't just stop doing everything on the list. Some of her resistance was habitual (i.e., this is how I've always done things). We could work to cut that stuff out immediately. But a number of activities on Michelle's list involved other people. She feared she might offend her colleagues if she expressed concern that some of their work together was pointless. I told her this was understandable. I asked about her level of confidence that she was accurately appraising the value of the activities on her list. "Oh, I'm pretty sure. Nearly all of this stuff is nonsense," she told me. I then asked if her colleagues might be thinking the same thing, if perhaps they were scared to confront her about all the nonsense for the same reasons she didn't want to confront them. Her eyes lit up. "I never really thought of it like that," she told me.

Over the next few weeks, Michelle initiated open and honest conversations with her coworkers. She was able to eliminate nearly 70 percent of the junk on her list. Not only did she feel freer and more present for what really mattered, but so did everyone on her team.

It's astonishing how much of our time, energy, and attention we devote toward tasks that do not serve us well. These may be habitual activities that were once useful but are no longer. Or, as was the case with Michelle, they may be endeavors that involve other people. Often, the only thing getting in the way of us not sinking our attention into these activities is ourselves. But we can change this, especially if we remember that the stakes are high. How we spend our hours is how we spend our days. And, as the writer Annie Dillard so eloquently pointed out, "How we spend our days is . . . how we spend our lives."

In chapter 2, we defined our core values and reflected on some of the actions that work in service of them. It's worth regularly asking yourself if you are directing your attention and energy in ways that align with these values. What changes can you make in your life, both personal and professional, so that you can spend less time on the shallow and more time on the meaningful? What seeds are you regularly watering that you don't want to be watering? How can you free up more of yourself to water the seeds that you do want to be watering? Consider making a list like Michelle's, and don't be scared to ruthlessly make cuts. While to-do lists can be beneficial, if they are unwieldy they impede upon presence, keeping us from productive activity and pointing us toward undiscerning productivity, or what Seneca called idle busyness, instead. When it comes to reclaiming your presence, creating a not-to-do list is usually more powerful.

FINAL THOUGHTS ON PRESENCE

Being present isn't just about being grounded in the here and now—that is, not being pushed and pulled around by endless distractions—but also about laying a foundation for the future. Presence allows you to actively direct your own personal evolution instead of going wherever the current takes you. It ensures that you are engaged in meaningful productive activity instead of thoughtless and inertia-driven productivity.

We also learned that when you are in flow—or long ago what the Buddha called Nirvana and the Taoists called the Way—time seems to evaporate altogether. This makes sense. When you are fully present you aren't thinking back or ahead. You are not worried about falling behind or everything else that you have to do. You are simply existing in the here and now. As a consequence, when you practice presence you tend to become less rushed and more patient. That is the principle of groundedness we'll turn to next.

4

BE PATIENT AND YOU'LL GET THERE FASTER

D onna began working for a Fortune 100 company straight out of college, in the early nineties. For two decades, she rose through the ranks, gradually moving into roles with increasing responsibility and accountability. In 2016, she got the biggest, and least expected, promotion of her career. She was invited to join the C-suite, where she would be one of just eight leaders in an organization with thousands of employees and offices across the globe. She would also be the only woman and the only African American on the leadership team, what some of her colleagues reverentially came to call the "double only." We met for our first coaching session shortly after she accepted the position. She told me that she couldn't have ever imagined this. "I just followed my interests and tried to work with good people. I'm an accidental executive, I guess," she said. "This all feels very surreal." Though Donna had held large leadership roles before, nothing compared to this.

Part of what catapulted Donna into her new position was her ability to see big projects through to their completion. She earned a reputation as someone who could push work along in a massive organization, and when it wasn't moving at the right pace, she'd insert herself to get the job done. She was a world-class doer; she had a serious knack for making things happen. This can be advantageous when you are leading ten, a hundred, or perhaps even a thousand people. But when you're leading tens of thousands of people, when you're at the helm of a massive ship and navigating constantly changing currents, the desire to make things happen can actually start to get in the way. In her new leadership position, every time Donna tried to force an issue, to drive something through, she ended up frustrated. She was stressed out, working endless hours, and hardly sleeping. Meanwhile, for all her efforts, the plans and projects she was trying to expedite usually didn't move any faster. If anything, some of them slowed down.

Donna experienced what so many of my executive coaching clients do when they first take on large leadership roles, and what all of us experience when we endeavor toward significant goals. We want results now. We want to feel comfortable and in control, to problem-solve and fix things. It is true that these attitudes, key components of heroic individualism, can be like rocket fuel in certain situations, propelling us forward at top speed. But in many other situations, they become counterproductive. To be effective and hold her center, Donna had to learn a new way of leadership, a new way of being. She had to learn to practice patience.

As you'll see, the type of patience I am referring to is not equivalent to waiting forever without results. Rather, it is a thoughtful and steady persistence that requires slowing down in the short term to go faster and farther in the long term. It is what Donna and I came to refer to as the difference between making things happen and letting things happen, the difference between stepping in and exerting your will and stepping back and allowing things to unfold on their own time. Though there is a time and place for both of these strategies, most people default to the former even when the latter is optimal.

The third principle of groundedness is *patience.* Patience neutralizes our inclination to hurry, rush, and overemphasize acute situations in favor of playing the long game. In doing so, it lends itself to stability, strength, and lasting progress.

SOMETIMES PATIENCE IS PAINFUL

In 2014, at the University of Virginia in Charlottesville, the social psychologist Timothy Wilson had a hunch that, perhaps more so than ever, people don't like waiting. To test his hypothesis, Wilson recruited hundreds of undergraduate students and community members to take part in what he told them were "thinking periods." Participants were placed in empty rooms for fifteen minutes without anything to distract them. Their smartphones, laptops, and notebooks were confiscated. Wilson gave the participants two options: sit and wait out the fifteen minutes, or shock themselves with a strong electrical current. The results were shocking—literally. Sixty-seven percent of men and 25 percent of women chose to shock themselves, often repeatedly, rather than sit still and wait. These weren't self-selected masochists. Before the study, all participants said that they would pay money to avoid shocking themselves.

But when it came to sitting and waiting—again, for a mere fifteen minutes—a majority of men and a sizable proportion of women preferred running electricity through their bodies.

Wilson's hypothesis was correct. The results of his study strongly demonstrate that people dislike boredom and struggle with waiting. Though the pains to which people in Wilson's study went to avoid waiting were surprising, the general theme is not. Our society emphasizes results now. We order food with the click of a button and expect it to arrive at our doorstep in minutes. We read 280-character tweets instead of long-form investigative reporting. We're constantly peddled a variety of quick fixes and "hacks." Heroic individualism craves instant wealth, instant health, and instant happiness. Some people even want to live forever, becoming obsessed with longevity—the irony is that they want it now and in a magic pill, diet, or some other kind of silver bullet or quick fix.

Research conducted by the firm Forrester shows that in 2006, online shoppers expected web pages to load in under four seconds. Three years later, that number was compressed to two seconds. By 2012, Google engineers learned that internet users expect search results to load within a mere two-fifths of a second, or about how long it takes to blink. There's no reason to believe this trend is slowing down. The author Nicholas Carr, whose book *The Shallows* explores the far-reaching effects of the internet, says, "As our technologies increase the intensity of stimulation and the flow of new things, we adapt to that pace. We become less patient. When moments without stimulation arise, we start to feel panicked and don't know what to do with them, because we've trained ourselves to expect this stimulation."

A prescient 2012 report, "Millennials Will Benefit and Suffer

Due to Their Hyperconnected Lives," conducted by the Pew Research Center's Internet and American Life Project, predicted that a side effect of our hyperconnected world is the "expectation of instant gratification." I write "side effect" because it's just that. There's nothing inherently bad about expedient technology—I rely on it, and I'm just as likely as the next person to become frustrated when the hourglass on whatever screen I happen to be looking at doesn't empty fast enough. But when we expect this kind of speed, ongoing stimulation, and instant gratification in other areas of our lives, it can become problematic.

Generally speaking, good things take time to come to fruition. Patience is an advantage in athletics, business, creativity, science, and relationships. Silicon Valley tells us to "move fast and break things." But, as evidenced by the failures and harmful unintended consequences of so many Silicon Valley companies, if you adopt that mindset, what you often end up is broken. Cultivating patience serves as a buffer against getting caught up in frenetic energy and angst. It helps offset the temptation to seek novelty always and constantly change course. It invites us to show up reliably and thoughtfully, even when things appear to be moving slowly. It encourages us to take a longer view, to recognize when it's wise to let situations unfold in their own time. It even helps us to move swiftly in the moment. One of my closest friends, Justin, is an emergency room doctor in downtown Oakland, California. His mantra during every-second-counts trauma cases: "Go slow to go fast."

Consider a topic that is at least somewhat familiar to most: diets. Drawn to the trendiest approaches, many people who strive to lose weight constantly bounce between fads: low-fat, low-carb, South Beach, Atkins, DASH, Zone, Ornish, keto, intermittent fasting . . .

the list goes on and on. It's not that these diets don't work. It's that the continual switching is detrimental to losing weight. A 2018 study out of Stanford University compared low-fat and low-carb diets, also tracking randomly assigned participants for a year. The best predictor of weight loss wasn't which diet the participants were assigned to but whether they adhered to that diet. Outside of reckless approaches, the best diet is the one to which you can stick. That's all there is to it. Easy to understand, but apparently hard to practice. Writing about these and other experimental nutrition results in *The New York Times*, Aaron Carroll, a physician researcher at the Indiana University School of Medicine, explains that "successful diets over the long haul are most likely ones that involve slow and steady changes."

Of course, it's not just diets. The same is true for just about any persistent change, whether it's in performance, health, or happiness. If you rush the process or expect results too swiftly, you'll end up repeatedly disappointed. The larger and more meaningful the endeavor, the more that patience is important. When I was in the thick of my experience with OCD, one of the best pieces of advice I received was from my psychiatrist, Dr. Lucas V.D. "Be patient," he told me. "It's a nine-inning game." Though I longed to be in the bottom of the ninth with a seven-run lead, the truth is that, at the time, I was probably still in the middle of the second inning. He set an expectation that recovery was going to be a long-term endeavor, a journey unfolding with ups and downs, with some innings that would be better than others. His advice really struck a chord with me. In so many areas of life—both personal and professional—we tend to zoom in and view the present moment as all-encompassing. It doesn't help that our culture reinforces this with its incessant focus on speed and overnight progress. But when we zoom out and realize that so many of the projects in our lives are nine-inning games, the perceived immediacy of whatever it is we are dealing with relaxes. And so does the distress that perceived immediacy causes. Challenging times become a little less challenging when we realize they won't last forever. Consequently, we can move forward with more thoughtfulness, consistency, and ultimately a greater chance of attaining a fulfilling kind of success that is a hallmark of groundedness.

NO SUCH THING AS AN OVERNIGHT BREAKTHROUGH

As a young geologist, Charles Darwin spent nearly five years on HMS *Beagle*, a large ship circumnavigating the globe on a far-reaching scientific expedition. Though the ship set sail in 1831, it wasn't until 1835, on a visit to the Galapagos Islands toward the end of the voyage, that Darwin began to formulate his theory of natural selection, which at the time was referred to as the transmutation of species. It took him more than four years at sea before his revolutionary insight began to take shape. But even this was only the beginning. Upon his return, Darwin worked vigorously on the theory, making significant gains between 1836 and 1838. Yet it was not until 1859 that he published his masterwork, *On the Origin of Species*. In other words, he spent more than twenty years working and reworking his ideas. During that time, Darwin overcame countless wrong turns, criticisms, and mental blocks. In his own words, he considered his success to be due chiefly to "the love of science, unbounded patience in long reflecting over any subject." Arguably the greatest scientific breakthrough of modern history wasn't really a breakthrough at all. It was over two decades in the making. When *On the Origin of Species* was first published twenty-eight years after Darwin set sail on HMS *Beagle*, Darwin, the provocative and unconventional trailblazer, was fifty years old.

Contrary to what the mindset of heroic individualism would make you think, progress is often slow, and that's okay. To make a meaningful difference in just about anything consequential, the work you put in needs to persist long enough to break through inevitable barriers and plateaus. What seems like a static period may not be a static period at all; you might just not be seeing the effects of your efforts yet. When you work on something significant, something significant is working on you. I've yet to meet someone who describes their happiest or most fulfilling moments as being hurried or rushed.

Intellectually, this all might sound good. In reality, however, plateaus can be especially frustrating. They expose all kinds of hidden motivations. Are you doing what you're doing because you are addicted to external results? Can you keep going without the constant dopamine (the feel-good neurochemical) hit that accompanies observable progress? Can you largely tune out a consumer culture trying to take you off course with endless promises of overnight success, hacks, and other enticing fads, shams, and quick fixes?

How you answer these questions is key to long-term success and fulfillment. Sometimes you need to pound the stone over and over again before it breaks. Remember, that doesn't mean your previous blows weren't working. The tension may very well be building, and you just can't see it yet. A breakthrough might be right around the corner.

"Sudden" breakthroughs are particularly common in athletic training, in which it's ordinary to go from running eight-minute miles for weeks and weeks and then suddenly drop down to 7:45. Or for your squat in the weight room to be stuck at 275 pounds for months, only to see it jump, seemingly overnight, to 305. Exercise scientists call this the cycle of compensation and supercompensation. It takes your body time to absorb and adapt to hard training. On a cellular level, the soonest you're likely to see the lasting benefits of a workout is ten days after that workout, and often it's much longer than that. Usually what happens is that athletes get a little bit worse before they get better. At more elite levels of sport, it's not uncommon for athletes to train for an entire year before realizing the targeted adaptations of their workouts. Their bodies are compensating for the workload—that is, staying the same or maybe even deteriorating a little as they recover and rebound from the stress of training—before supercompensating, or becoming stronger in observable ways.

It's not just athletics that follows this pattern. A 2018 study published in the prestigious journal *Nature* examined performance in creative and intellectual pursuits. The researchers found that while most people have a "hot streak" in their career—"a specific period during which an individual's performance is substantially better than his or her typical performance"—the timing is somewhat unpredictable. "The hot streak emerges randomly within an individual's sequence of works, is temporally localized, and is not associated with any detectable change in productivity," the researchers write. But one thing just about every hot streak has in common?

They all rest on a foundation of prior work, during which observable improvement was much less substantial. If these individuals had given up, left their careers, or switched approaches too early, their breakthroughs would not have occurred. They had to practice patience. Vincent van Gogh produced more than twenty paintings in 1888, just two years before his death. These paintings included two of his most famous works, *The Starry Night* and *Sunflowers*.

Another example of patience and persistence leading to a groundbreaking hot streak is Ta-Nehisi Coates. As a young writer, Coates fought to survive early in his career. From 1996 to 2008, he bounced around various publications. When his first book, *The Beautiful Struggle*, was published in 2008, hardly anyone noticed. By then Coates had lost three jobs, and to stay afloat his family was reliant on unemployment checks, his wife's income, and support from relatives. But Coates kept grinding. In 2008, he landed an online column with *The Atlantic*, which slowly but surely gained traction and an avid readership. But it wasn't until 2012, nearly two decades and hundreds of stories into his career, that Coates fully hit his stride. That year, he wrote the *Atlantic* cover story "Fear of a Black President." In 2014, his essay "The Case for Reparations" became one of the most widely read and discussed pieces on the internet. And in 2015, his second book, *Between the World and Me*, was a number one *New York Times* bestseller and Pulitzer Prize finalist. Even more important, it inarguably changed the national—and perhaps even international—discourse on race. In 2017, a few days before his forty-second birthday, the *Times* called Coates "one of the most influential black intellectuals of his generation."

Speaking to young writers on the importance of eliminating distractions and practicing patience, Coates offered, "What all of this leads to is being able to see as much of the world as possible, but you need time to see the world. You so need time. And you don't want to cultivate things that rob you of time." When asked about creative breakthrough, he said, "It's not really that mystical—it's like repeated practice over and over and over again, and then suddenly you become something you had no idea you could really be." As I write this in 2020, amid a large movement for social justice, Coates's work is cited pretty much everywhere, multiple times per week. His patience and persistence not only allowed him to transform himself. It's also helping to transform the world.

Perhaps the most surprising arena in which patience is a substantial advantage is in technology and at cutting-edge companies. We tend to associate start-up culture with heroic individualism, speed, and youth. But this association is false. Mark Zuckerberg, the founder and CEO of Facebook, once said of entrepreneurs: "I want to stress the importance of being young and technical. Young people are just smarter." However, Zuckerberg, who offered this wisdom when he was in his late twenties, is wrong.

We know this for certain thanks to researchers from the MIT Sloan School of Management. In a substantial study, they examined all businesses launched in the United States between 2007 and 2014, a data set that encompassed 2.7 million founders. They compared a founder's age to a variety of company performance measures, such as employment, sales growth, and when relevant, a company's value at initial public offering (IPO). What they found is that successful entrepreneurs are much more likely to be middle-aged than young. For the top 0.1 percent of the fastest-growing businesses in America during their study window, the average age of the founder when their company was first launched is forty-five. Middle-aged founders also have the most successful IPOs. A fifty-year-old founder is 1.8 times more likely than a thirty-year-old founder to create a high-growth business. Even those who start their companies when they are young may not peak until later in life, according to the Sloan researchers. The iPhone, arguably Steve Jobs's and Apple's most innovative product, hit the market when Jobs was fifty-two, two years older than Darwin was when *On the Origin of Species* was first published.

It cannot be overlooked that there are risks associated with doing the same thing that you've always done without seeing any change—be it in the gym, the workplace, or a relationship. As the science writer David Epstein pointed out in his book *Range*, sometimes we spend too much time grinding it out when we'd be wiser to switch and find something more suited to our interests and skills. This is especially true when we first throw ourselves into new disciplines. Economists call this *match quality*—or one's fit for certain types of activities and work. Epstein makes a compelling case that match quality is even more important than grit. After all, if you're a good fit for what you're doing, then you're likely to stick with it.*

But once you have already established match quality there is often an equal, if not greater, risk in stopping or changing your approach prematurely. Based on my own experience and an informal survey of my coaching colleagues—those who work with athletes, executives, and creatives—giving up on something too soon is far

---

*A personal example to drive this home: I have always been a particularly gritty writer, overcoming countless obstacles and failures all the way back to primary school, during which I was told I couldn't write. These failures continued through high school and culminated in me getting rejected from journalism school. (And, of course, also in my having countless essays and articles turned down, which happens with great frequency to this day.) But I have never shown grit in science or math. This doesn't mean I am—or am not—a gritty person. It simply means I like writing a lot more than I like science or math. Writing offers much better match quality for me. As a result, here we are.

more common than waiting around too long. This isn't surprising. Humans suffer from what behavioral scientists call the *commission bias*, or the tendency to err on the side of action over inaction. If we don't see results, we get impatient and feel a strong urge to do something—anything—to expedite our progress. But often the best thing we can do is nothing—staying the course, tweaking as we go, and letting things unfold in their own time. Instead of always thinking, *Don't just stand there, do something*, we should at least consider thinking, *Don't just do something, stand there.*

CONSISTENCY COMPOUNDS

The truth about progress is this: when you don't rush the process, when you take small and consistent steps over time, you give yourself the best chance to end up with massive gains. Someone who knows this well is Stanford professor BJ Fogg, one of the world's preeminent experts on human behavior. In Fogg's model of human progress, whether someone takes a desired action depends on both their motivation and their ability to complete a given task. Regardless of your motivation, if you regularly overshoot with respect to your ability, trying to do too much too soon, you're liable to become discouraged and quickly flame out. Or maybe you'll frequently get injured—emotionally or physically. But if you incrementally increase the challenge, what was hard last week will seem easier today. Put differently, habits build upon themselves. Small and consistent victories compound over time. This doesn't mean that progress is always linear. You'll have good days and bad days. What you want is for your average to become better.

We see a powerful example of patience and raising your average in finance. There's an underused (perhaps because it requires patience) investment philosophy known as *dollar-cost averaging*. The basic theory goes like this: Put a little money into a large fund every day. When the market is down, you'll be buying more shares. When the market is up, you'll be buying fewer shares. Dollar-cost averaging takes advantage of what statisticians call regression toward the mean, or the short-term tendency of any dynamic system to return to its average state.

In the long term, so long as the market gradually goes up—in essence, an incrementally increasing average—you create wealth. This philosophy applies to areas of life far beyond investing. A strategy superior to putting forth occasional heroic efforts and burning out is focusing on consistency and improving the average over time. This requires showing up not only on your good days but on your bad days, too. Adopting a mindset that favors consistent small steps may take the excitement out of experiencing massive highs and lows, but it leads to more enduring progress. It also spawns a greater sense of stability and ease, which next I'll argue is more fulfilling than excitement anyway.

EASE VERSUS EXCITEMENT

Eliud Kipchoge is a Kenyan runner who in 2018 shattered the marathon world record. He is the best in the world at what he does. In addition to being supremely fast, he is supremely thoughtful. He's been given the nickname "the philosopher king of running."

When asked about his recipe for success, Kipchoge answers that the key is not overextending himself in training. He is not fanatical about trying to be great all the time. He is, however, consistent and patient. For example, he has trained with the same coach for more than a decade in a sport where most athletes frequently switch. Shortly before setting his world record, Kipchoge told *The New York Times* that he rarely, if ever, pushes himself past 80 percent—90 percent at most—of his maximum effort during workouts. This allows him to string together weeks of consistent training. He is a master of letting things happen in their own time instead of trying to make them happen. His coach, Patrick Sang, says that the secret to Kipchoge's speed is that he makes progress "slowly by slowly."

For his part, Kipchoge told the *Times*, "I want to run with a relaxed mind." And in this regard, he does exactly what he wants.

Perhaps even more so than his speed, Kipchoge is known for his ease, both on and off the road. On the road, his stride is smooth as silk and he almost always runs with a smile on his face, even toward the end of grueling races. When other runners are visibly suffering, their faces grimacing and strides becoming robotic and breaking down, Kipchoge appears to be gliding effortlessly. Off the road, he speaks slowly and softly. Whereas other runners are preoccupied with trying to win races and set records, Kipchoge is not. For instance, when prodded about his goals prior to his world-record-setting race, Kipchoge shrugged his shoulders and informed the media: "To be precise, I am just going to try to run my personal best. If it comes as a world record, I would appreciate it."

Ease is often a by-product of patience (and of presence too; as mentioned earlier, these principles go hand in hand). Ease manifests when you are fully in the moment, letting things happen on their own time, neither forcing nor rushing your process. Excitement has a different texture. Excitement is contracting; it narrows your world. Your focus is on what comes next, always a few steps ahead of where you are. Excitement temporarily feels good. And there is no doubt that bursts of excitement add texture to your life. But if you are obsessively trying to generate the feeling, you may miss out on what is in front of you because you are already moving ahead. Ease, on the other hand, is expansive. Time slows and space widens. "We must distinguish happiness from excitement," writes Zen master Thich Nhat Hanh. "Many people think of excitement as happiness. They are thinking of something, or expecting something that they consider to be happiness, and for them, that is already happiness. But when you are excited you are not peaceful. True happiness is based on peace."

I've come to learn firsthand the difference between speed-charged excitement and patience-grounded ease. One morning, back when he was still an infant, my son showed an intense interest in a soft, bouncy blue ball. Perhaps he wanted to play a modified, eight-month-old version of catch, I thought to myself. As a lifelong athlete, I became very excited. But what was really happening was that *I* wanted him to play an eight-month-old version of catch. And in my excitement, I wanted it to happen now. I thought that if I encouraged him and demonstrated catch in every way imaginable he'd come along. But he wasn't interested. After about five minutes it hit me. My son was having a great time just being with the ball in his own way. Sucking on it. Looking at it. Touching it. Trying to eat it. Being awed when it rolled after he let go of it. I was so busy being excited about what could transpire, trying to control the situation, trying to make a game of catch happen, that I was missing out on the chance to watch my son be himself. Once I released myself from any notion of playing catch, from excitement about what might lie ahead, my entire experience changed. I became less tense, restless, and restricted. I became more present and open to experiencing what was in front of me, even if it wasn't anything close to a game of catch. I went from thinking about what could happen next to being with what was happening now. I transitioned from excitement to ease, from speed and thinking ahead to patience and presence now.

This made me reflect that I, and so many of the driven people I know, favor excitement over ease all the time. We close in on something because we want it to go a certain way, because we get excited about what *could* happen. This works in our favor enough, at least if you define favor as achieving quick and measurable results, that it becomes somewhat habitual. The problem is that excitement often comes at the expense of joy and ease. It pushes us in the direction of trying to control and make things happen when we'd be better off *letting* them happen instead.

It's worth being explicit that this does not mean you should never harness speed and excitement. It's just that you should also consider what you are giving up as a result. Perhaps your proverbial stone is about to break with just a few more blows. Maybe you are chronically missing out on the ease that comes with being patient and present for what is unfolding right now. We do things quickly—not better, but quickly—to gain time. But what's the point if in the time we gain we just do more things quickly? I have yet to meet someone who wants their headstone to read, "He rushed."

PRACTICE: LET THINGS HAPPEN INSTEAD OF ALWAYS TRYING TO MAKE THEM HAPPEN

Donna, the "accidental executive" with whom we opened this chapter, learned to step back from intervening in big projects when it was appropriate to do so. Whenever she felt a strong urge to lean in and make things happen, she used that urge as a cue to ask herself what might happen if she didn't. In some cases, the answer was chaos; in those instances she forced the issue, and rightfully so. But most of the time, it simply meant that the project or initiative would progress a bit differently, but no worse, than if she had inserted herself. The more comfortable she became stepping back, the more at ease she felt. She performed better, too. She realized that sometimes projects had to move slowly today so that they could move faster and more efficiently tomorrow. Donna grew into her role splendidly, becoming one of the most grounded leaders I've known. She's weathered countless ups and downs by taking a long view, by remembering that most of the significant ventures in our lives, both personal and professional, tend to be nine-inning games.

While coaching Donna through her leadership transition, I kept in mind a concept called the *good enough mother*. It was developed in the early 1950s by the psychoanalyst D. W. Winnicott. I'll update and use "good enough parent" from here on out. According to Winnicott, the good enough parent does not respond to their child's each and every need. They do not helicopter-parent, but they do not neglect their child either. Rather, the work of a good enough parent is to create a safe space for their child to develop and unfold on their own. There are certainly times when the good enough parent ought to lean in. But that's not the goal. The goal is to create a container in which the process—in this case, the growing child—can unfold on its own. Winnicott's work pointed out that leaning in comes easily to most parents. But learning to lean out requires deliberate effort.

For many of the big projects in our lives—including our own unfolding, and certainly raising children—it can be helpful to adopt the mindset of a good enough parent. This is especially true if we have a tendency toward rushing and making things happen, toward leaning in even when we'd be better off slowing down and leaning out. When you feel the urge to intervene by taking expedited action, ask yourself what it would look like to slow down whatever it is you are doing by 10 percent. What would it look like to take a soft step back and let things unfold on their own time for a bit longer? (This practice can be used on a smaller scale, too, like holding off on sending an email.) Sometimes it *does* make sense to intervene. This pause—and more generally, adopting the mindset of a good enough parent—simply helps you bring discernment to that decision instead of going forward on autopilot. It helps to break the pattern of running around in circles and subsequent stress in favor of more grounded being *and* doing.

PRACTICE: PROCESS OVER OUTCOMES— TAKE SMALL STEPS FOR BIG GAINS

One of the most popular Taoist texts is the *Tao Te Ching*. It was written in the sixth century BC by Lao-tzu, who is thought to be an older contemporary of Confucius. Occasionally Lao-tzu is referenced as a passive hermit. But according to the Taoist scholar Stephen Mitchell, this is a misperception arising from Lao-tzu's insistence on *wei wu wei*, literally translated as "doing not doing." If you closely read the *Tao Te Ching* you'll learn that Lao-tzu offered all kinds of advice for taking action in the world. It's just that the kind of action he championed was to be undertaken slowly, steadily, and harmoniously. He advised paying close attention to the flow of life, being patient, and taking consistent attainable steps instead of attempting intrepid efforts and failing. The master, wrote Lao-tzu, "accomplish[es] the great task by a series of small acts."

When you set big goals, it is easy to become overly excited about reaching them and, as a result, rush your process because you are so consumed by achieving a desired outcome. Sometimes, this even leads to reckless behavior. For an athlete it can result in injury, illness, and overtraining. For a traditional workplace professional it can result in burnout. In a Harvard Business School working paper titled "Goals Gone Wild: The Systematic Side Effects of Over-Prescribing Goal Setting," a team of researchers from Harvard, Northwestern, and the University of Pennsylvania set out to explore the potential downside of goal setting. They found that over-emphasizing goals—especially those that are based on measurable outcomes—often leads to reduced motivation, irrational risk-taking, and unethical behavior.

Rather than focusing on the heroic achievement of big goals, practice breaking them down into their component parts and then concentrate on those parts. Doing so serves as an incredibly powerful focusing mechanism. It keeps you present in the here and now and thus keeps you patient, even in the pursuit of distant goals. If you are concentrating on the work that is in front of you, you will be better off. This attitude, what I have come to call a *process mindset*, helps prevent you from trying to rush toward an outcome when taking your time is a better strategy. For most consequential endeavors, long-term progress is less about heroic effort and more about smart pacing; less about intensity on any given day and more about discipline over the course of months, and in some cases even years.

Cultivate a Process Mindset

- First, set a goal.

- Next, figure out the discrete steps to achieving that goal that are within your control.

- Then, mostly forget about the goal and focus on executing those steps instead. Judge yourself based on your level of presence and the effort you are exerting in the moment.

- If you catch yourself obsessing about the goal, use that as a cue to ask yourself what you could be doing *right now* to help you achieve it. Sometimes the answer may be nothing at all—resting.

- Throughout your process, remember that doing stuff for the sake of doing stuff isn't progress. It's just doing stuff.

PRACTICE: STOP ONE REP SHORT

Stopping one rep short is an old adage used by wise athletic coaches. It means ending your workout when you still have one more lap, lift, or mile in the tank. Though it is tempting to keep pushing—to do that extra set of sprints, for example—contrary to what heroic individualism might have you think, you can't constantly be going to the well and destroying yourself. You need to be able to pick up the next workout where you left off. What you are able to accomplish tomorrow is in part influenced by the restraint you show today. This strategy applies well beyond sports. For example, a common piece of writing advice is to stop one sentence short, to end a block of writing when you are still in the flow of things so that you can more easily pick up and then settle into a rhythm in your next session. The general practice goes like this:

- Identify areas of your life where a lack of patience has caused you problems—perhaps injury, illness, or burnout—in the past.

- Instead of doing what you're accustomed to doing, what you may want to do in the moment, force yourself to stop the equivalent of one rep short, day in and day out.

Stopping one rep short requires discipline. You need confidence in your process, confidence that if you stay patient, show restraint when appropriate, and take consistent small steps, you'll end up with big gains. Research published in the *British Journal of Sports Medicine* shows that most sports injuries happen when an athlete increases their training load too quickly. The best way to avoid injury is to slowly build up training volume over time. When acute workload, or what you did this week, is more than twice as much as chronic workload, or the average of what you've done the past four weeks, you're significantly more likely to sustain an injury versus when you make a more modest increase in training volume and intensity. Though the exact sweet spot for increasing workload is a matter of scientific debate, the general theme is that you don't want to increase any given day's workload to be that much greater than the average of the past month's. I've seen this same principle apply in my executive coaching practice. When people take on too much too soon, or convince themselves that they can suddenly leap upward in output, symptoms of burnout usually loom around the corner.

Even so, stopping one rep short is one of the hardest things to do, especially for driven people. The vast majority of my own injuries (in sports) and periods of stagnation (in the creative process) have come as a result of disregarding this practice. That's a long-winded way of saying that I get it, I really do. I've found it can be helpful to enlist colleagues and friends to help hold you accountable. Think like the record-holding runner Kipchoge. Progress happens slowly by slowly. If you're prone to getting caught up in excitement and speed today, overshooting the target only to end up frustrated or feeling burnt out tomorrow, paste these words—*slowly by slowly*—in your work space, whether it's an office, an artist's studio, a classroom, or a garage gym.

PRACTICE: LEAVE YOUR PHONE BEHIND

In chapter 3, we discussed the benefits of eliminating distractions like digital devices to help usher in planned periods of presence. But you can also practice leaving your phone or other digital devices behind when you go about the usual activities of your day. For example, consider leaving your phone in the car when you go into the grocery store. If you end up having to wait in a checkout line for a few minutes, you'll be forced to practice patience. Two common barriers to this practice are:

1. It is easy and therefore not worth doing.

2. Why would I force downtime when I could be catching up on current events, text messages, social media, or my inbox?

The first barrier we know is not true, thanks to the University of Virginia study that found people would rather shock themselves with electricity than wait alone with nothing to do. Scrolling on your phone is a lot less painful than an electric shock. (It would, however, be interesting to see what would happen if people waiting in line didn't have their phones but did have the ability to shock themselves.)

To the second barrier, I would offer that the benefits of training patience far outweigh the perceived costs of not responding to a message immediately or potentially falling behind on current events, especially since so much "breaking" news is really just junk entertainment dressed up as something important. Not having our phones during short periods of waiting helps to decondition our addiction to stimulation, novelty, and speed. This carries over into larger aspects of life. The less we depend on novelty and speed, the more we can make intentional decisions about when to seek newness and move fast versus when to stay put and slow down.

Leaving your phone behind also provides you the opportunity to be more present for what you're doing. Remember, patience and presence go hand in hand. In the grocery store, for example, you might have a creative idea while waiting in the checkout line. You could also look the cashier in the eye, smile, and make a social connection, which in most cases is hugely beneficial to everyone involved. A few other ideas for when to leave your phone behind and develop patience and presence instead:

- Running errands

- Going on walks

- Going to the gym

- Using the bathroom (This is a hard one)

You don't have to do these always, and there are many other examples that might work better for you. The point is that you want to identify at least a few moments in your daily life when you can unplug and step back from speed and unrelenting novelty.

PRACTICE: THREE-BY-FIVE BREATHING

Like the other principles of groundedness, patience is a skill that needs to be developed. You cannot just think your way to being patient. There is no switch you can flip. Developing patience takes patience, making it that much harder if you are accustomed to speed and quick fixes. A simple but effective exercise is to regularly practice pausing. A modest way to do this is to close your eyes and take five deep breaths three times a day. You can pair these breaths with specific activities, like eating dinner, showering, brushing your teeth, or prior to checking your phone in the morning. Your only job is to follow each breath all the way in and all the way out.

This may be the most straightforward practice in the entire book, but that doesn't mean it's easy. If you are habituated to speed, pausing for even just a minute, which is all this exercise takes, can feel like an uncomfortable eternity, particularly at first. If by the time you've taken just two breaths you observe yourself feeling restless or rushed, simply note what is happening and then return to the sensation of the breath, without judging yourself for drifting away. If you keep up with this practice you'll start to become more comfortable with it. You'll also find that it carries over into other parts of your day, too, helping you to experience the openness and stability of ease when you'd otherwise feel tight, contracted, anxious, and rushed.

As mentioned earlier, the ability to pause is additionally beneficial when you feel a desire to switch approaches or make significant changes. Remember, humans are prone to the commission bias, or a predisposition toward action over inaction. We tend to ask ourselves what we might get from making a change or taking an action, but we don't ask ourselves what we might give up. All it takes is a brief pause to consider the latter. There is no right answer, and it will depend on the unique circumstances of your situation. The key is pausing to consider the question. In this way, pausing is not just about learning to be more patient in the now, but also about supporting you to take a long and more thoughtful view toward the future.

FINAL THOUGHTS ON PATIENCE

There is one final reason why we tend toward speed over patience. Speed can be a defense mechanism. Ceaselessly moving fast and getting swept up in heroic individualism's propensity to look outward helps us avoid confronting the things we fear most. But no amount of frenetic activity will make them go away. Try as we might, we cannot outrun these fears. They will always catch up. These include what for many is the fear underlying all others: our own mortality, a particularly hard concept to face.

In ancient Buddhist texts, there is a parable about a strident deity called Rohitassa, who viewed himself as a hero. On one occasion, Rohitassa asked the Buddha: "Do you think it is possible to escape this world of birth and death, of suffering and discrimination, by means of speed?"

The Buddha responded, "No, Rohitassa. It is not possible to escape this world by traveling, even at great speed."

Rohitassa said, "Right you are. In a previous life I traveled extremely fast, as fast as the speed of light. I didn't eat, sleep, didn't drink. I did nothing but travel at great speed and I still could not get out of this world. In the end, I died before I could do so."

Moving at warp speed neither gets us where we want to go nor provides us with strength or stability. There is nothing heroic about quick fixes, hacks, or silver bullets, especially given they rarely, if ever, work. Most breakthroughs rest upon a long-standing foundation of steady and consistent effort. For so many of the meaningful endeavors in our lives, the best way to move fast is to go about it slowly, to proceed with a gentle yet firm persistence. Modern science, ancient wisdom, and the practice of highly fulfilled peak performers shows us this is true. When we proceed with patience, our output becomes more sustainable over the long haul. We also tend to have a better experience along the way. We become less contracted and more open, less hurried and more present. And while transitioning from speed to patience may require us to confront our fears, this is not problematic. As you'll see in the next chapter, when we confront our fears we develop deeper trust and confidence within ourselves, and we also forge connections with others. By opening up to and exploring our cracks we become more solid. Vulnerability—the root of which, *vulnus*, literally means "wound"—requires strength. And strength requires vulnerability.

5

EMBRACE VULNERABILITY TO DEVELOP GENUINE STRENGTH AND CONFIDENCE

hen my OCD first manifested, I was beginning to establish myself as an expert on human performance, with writing and citations in prestigious outlets like *The New York Times*, *The Wall Street Journal*, NPR, *Forbes*, and *Wired*. During an especially rough evening, I received an email from a young man asking how I had achieved so much and crafted such a compelling life at just thirty-one years old. Little did he know that I had spent most of that day filled with angst, struggling with thoughts of how life was utterly meaningless. I was in one of OCD's vicious loops: a distressing thought followed by an awful feeling; fighting against that thought and feeling; having them come back stronger; repeat ad infinitum. When I read this young man's email I nearly broke down. I felt like an impostor, a fraud, like I was living a double life. Performance expert and author on the outside, but a complete wreck and falling to pieces on the inside.

Though my experience of living a double life, which I'll say a bit more about soon, may be a bit extreme, this feeling is not uncommon. Though this feeling is as old as time, it has intensified thanks to the internet and social media, where people "show up" as if everything in their lives is perfect. Researchers from Stanford University found that social media portrays a too-rosy view. Most social media users selectively filter what to share, the researchers explain, and then further edit those preselected images and events to make them seem even better and more attractive. For example, the new parent who shares something about their perfect baby while holding back the sleepless nights, second-guessing, lack of intimacy with their partner, and strain on their marriage. Or the business professional who posts on LinkedIn about their project's massive success without mentioning the angst, burnout, and destructive toll it has had on their relationships. As a result of this selective sharing, many believe that they are alone in their difficulties. Everyone else, it seems, is living fantastic and blissful lives. This misperception leads to even further distress for all involved because it creates a cycle in which users never feel like their lives are good enough, so they post increasingly filtered and edited updates and tell themselves increasingly filtered and edited stories about themselves—in essence, keeping up with the digital Joneses. Given that so many social media users are doing this, the entire experience can become an upward spiral of living a facade, leaving both the poster and viewer (most people play both roles on the same day) feeling worse off.

Of course this cycle isn't just confined to social media. Trying to live up to an inflated persona—and not only your online self, but your workplace self, the self you bring to community events, and even sometimes the perfect story you tell yourself about yourself—creates what psychologists call *cognitive dissonance*, or an inconsistency between who you portray yourself to be and who you really are. In his 1959 book, *The Presentation of Self in Everyday Life*, the sociologist Erving Goffman delineated what he called our "front stage" and our "backstage" selves. Our front stage selves are the ones we bring to social situations or when we're trying to delude ourselves. They tend to be performative, as if we are playing a specific role for an audience. Our backstage selves represent who we are when we stop acting, when we don't consider how we'll be perceived by others or measure ourselves against some kind of arbitrary bar of perfection, against the illusory standard of heroic individualism. Our front stage and backstage selves are not binary. Most human behavior lies on a spectrum between these two extremes. But when someone spends too much time playing their front stage self, particularly when there is a wide gap between their front stage and backstage selves, distress usually follows.

Distress is something that I didn't need any more of in my life. So, shortly after receiving that email from the young man asking for the secret to my success, I decided to share my experience of OCD with the public. Did I want to help other people who might be suffering in silence? Of course. But more than anything, I wanted to create coherence in my identity. I wrote a long essay for *Outside* in which I spilled my guts. I put everything out there. Large chunks of the essay got cut because my editor was concerned about their

THE PRACTICE OF GROUNDEDNESS

effect on others suffering alone with mental illness. But here are a few parts that made it to print:

> *A particularly distressing moment occurred on a long car ride last October. Out of nowhere, I was pummeled by the thought, "You should just drive off the road and end it all right now. Your family will be fine without you." It was as if I had become the thought and there was nothing I could do to escape. I knew somewhere deep down inside that I didn't really want to kill myself; I had just enough self-awareness to realize these thoughts and feelings made no sense. But I would have given anything short of my life for the suffering to end. It was so painful. That drive was the hardest four hours of my life. I was terrified for days—terrified to get in a car, terrified to be around sharp objects, terrified to be alone. . . . My anxiety took over my life. It was the only thing I could think about. Sometimes it still is. . . .*
>
> *It's hard to come to terms with an illness that affects my mind. When I injure my body, it's easy to say, "my calf is pulled" or "I have a stress fracture in my heel." But if I don't have control over my mind, I can't help but wonder who am "I." It's also hard to reconcile being an "expert" on performance and experiencing what I'm experiencing. At times, I feel like a fraud and an imposter, fragile and scared.**

Writing and publishing this essay was hard, no doubt. But it was much easier than going on feeling like a fraud. The piece quickly became my most read ever. I received hundreds of emails from

---

*Brad Stulberg, "When a Stress Expert Battles Mental Illness," *Outside*, March 7, 2018.

people who shared with me their stories of mental illness, including many from those who are world-class at what they do. (There's a lesson here: everyone, and I mean everyone, faces challenges and goes through dark, trying times.) It was not my intention to write a popular story. I just wanted to be real—real with myself and real with others. My impetus for writing about my OCD was primarily to rid myself of the distress caused by my split identity, to lessen the cognitive dissonance, the gap between my front stage and backstage selves, to make it a bit easier to heal.

Throughout this ordeal I learned an important lesson. I needed to stop trying so damn hard to be invincible, to live up to any notion of heroic individualism, and instead just be myself.

The fourth principle of groundedness is *vulnerability*. It is about being honest with yourself and others, even—and especially—when that means confronting perceived weaknesses and fears. Vulnerability has long been part of traditions like Buddhism, Stoicism, and Taoism. Common to all of these traditions is an emphasis on digging deep and exploring your inner experience: opening to the good, the bad, the beautiful, and the ugly. These traditions teach that facing your vulnerabilities helps you to more fully know and trust yourself, and to forge close and nourishing bonds with others. The thirteenth-century mystic Meister Eckhart taught that where you think you are weak you are strong, and where you think you are strong you are weak. As you'll see in the coming pages, the more you grapple with, open up to, and share your vulnerabilities, the more solid and grounded you become. It can be helpful to think of vulnerabilities as cracks. The way that you fill them is by facing them and, when appropriate, revealing them.

LEARNING TO TRUST YOURSELF

Opening yourself up to all of your experiences is hard, and some-times even terrifying, work. It can be distressing to discover parts of yourself that are less than perfect, that are more fragile than they are strong. "In all my research's two-hundred-thousand-plus pieces of data, I can't find a single example of courage that didn't require vulnerability. . . . Can you think of one moment of courage that didn't require risk, uncertainty, and emotional exposure?" writes the University of Houston researcher Brené Brown in her book *Braving the Wilderness*. But according to Brown, the more familiar you become with these parts of yourself and the more you learn to accept them, the better off you will be. Brown's research shows that embracing vulnerability increases self-worth, builds intimacy in relationships (including with yourself), aids in innova-tion, and elicits compassion. Plus, when it comes to being vulnera-ble, it's not really like you have a choice, at least not if you yearn to live a fulfilled life.

A few years ago, I went to see the poet and philosopher David Whyte speak. I left the event with the following scribbled in my notebook: *The things you care about make you vulnerable. The things you care about break your heart.*

It's hard to care—to really care—be it about a person, a pursuit, or a movement. Things don't always go the way you want them to, and they always change. The kids move out. Your body ages and you're forced to retire. You lose the race. The project goes down the drain. The movement fails to accomplish its aim. Your partner of twenty years receives a cancer diagnosis. Your partner of thirty years dies. This is just how it goes.

A common defense is to prevent yourself from caring. To coast instead of giving it your all. To put up a wall around your heart, a barrier between the deepest parts of you and the world. Perhaps the hurt isn't as intense this way. But neither are the joys. You miss out on a lot of richness. <u>A full life requires vulnerability.</u>

"Vulnerability is not a weakness, a passing indisposition, or something we can arrange to do without," writes Whyte. "Vulnerability is not a choice. Vulnerability is the underlying, ever-present, and abiding undercurrent of our natural state. To run from vulnerability is to run from the essence of our nature."

When you stop running, however hard it may be, there are no longer parts of you that are unfamiliar. You come to know all of yourself. And when you come to know all of yourself, you come to trust all of yourself too. Out of this trust emerges genuine strength and confidence. "I want to unfold," writes the poet Rainer Maria Rilke. "I don't want to stay folded anywhere. Because where I am folded, there I am a lie."

Where there is resistance, suppression, or delusion there is fragility, unfilled cracks in your ground. As we learned in chapter 2, the things we push away tend to grow stronger, even if only under the surface. But we cannot push these things down forever. Eventually, they arise and shake us to the core.

VULNERABILITY BENEFITS EVERYONE

On November 5, 2017, the NBA's Cleveland Cavaliers were matched up against the Atlanta Hawks. At the end of the first half, the Cavaliers were trailing 54 to 45. Kevin Love, the Cavaliers' twenty-nine-year-old, six-foot-eight power forward, had a relatively quiet first half. He scored just four points and made four rebounds, well below his averages. Love felt off. He couldn't pinpoint the issue, but on that night he wasn't himself. Early in the second half, when the Cavaliers' coach, Tyronn Lue, called a timeout, Love arrived at the bench short of breath. His mouth suddenly dried and his heart rate spiked. Unsure of what was happening, Love ran off the floor and into the locker room. His distress built upon itself, quickly getting worse. He ended up on the floor in the training room, lying on his back, gasping for air, thinking he was going to die. He struggles to remember what happened next. Team officials rushed him to the Cleveland Clinic, where doctors ran extensive medical testing on him. Everything checked out fine. Yes, Love was relieved. But even more so he was confused. What had happened?

Love later learned that he had experienced a massive panic attack. Panic attacks are common; research published in the journal *Archives of General Psychiatry* shows that 22.7 percent of people experience one at some point during their lives. Of those who experience an isolated attack, most have a crappy and worrisome few days and then get on with their usual routine. Yet a small number go on to develop a long-standing form of anxiety, joining the 18 percent of American adults who have an anxiety disorder and the 2 to 4 percent who suffer from more severe varieties. Love was concerned about falling into the latter category. Writing in *The Players' Tribune*, he expressed, "I couldn't bury what had happened and try to move forward. As much as part of me wanted to, I couldn't allow myself to dismiss the panic attack and everything underneath it. I didn't want to have to deal with everything sometime in the future, when it might be worse. I knew that much." So Love did what at the time was unheard of for an NBA tough guy. He faced his vulnerabilities and saw a therapist.

Though he was skeptical at first, he quickly grasped the value. "I realized how many issues come from places that you may not realize until you really look into them. I think it's easy to assume we know ourselves, but once you peel back the layers it's amazing how much there is to still discover," he wrote in *The Players' Tribune*. When Love peered deeply into himself, he saw how much his grandmother Carol's death had affected him, and how he had been pushing down those emotions. Carol had played a formative role in Love's upbringing. When she died in 2013, he was emerging as an NBA star, and the pace of the season left him little time to grieve her loss. Love described the process of opening up about his grandmother as "terrifying and awkward and hard." But over time, the more Love went to the places of sorrow and confusing emotions, the places he feared most, the more stable he felt. "I want to make it clear that I don't have things figured out about all of this. I'm just starting to do the hard work of getting to know myself. For 29 years, I avoided that. Now, I'm trying to be truthful with myself," he writes. "I'm trying to face the uncomfortable stuff in life while also enjoying, and being grateful for, the good stuff. I'm trying to embrace it all, the good, bad and ugly."

Love isn't alone. A month before Love wrote about his experience with panic and anxiety in *The Players' Tribune*, shortly after midnight two days before he was set to start in the league's All-Star Game, then–Toronto Raptors shooting guard DeMar DeRozan tweeted, "This depression get the best of me . . ." And with those seven words, the twenty-eight-year-old DeRozan, known as a reserved introvert, began to open up to himself and the world about his mental health challenges. "It's one of them things that no matter how indestructible we look like we are, we're all human at the end of the day," he told the *Toronto Star*. "It's not nothing I'm against or ashamed of. Now, at my age, I understand how many people go through it. Even if it's just somebody can look at it like, 'He goes through it and he's still out there being successful and doing this,' I'm OK with that." DeRozan was confronting his depression at its darkest and loneliest hour, and giving others permission to do the same. He and Love were going to their weak spots to become stronger.

FACING FEARS

In Greek mythology, the god Pan resided just beyond the safe zone and village boundary. When humans mistakenly wandered into his space, they would be overcome with panic, fear, and dread. When they tried to escape, even the most trivial obstacles—small sticks and stones, little holes in the ground, gusts of wind—would elicit paralyzing fear, and in their fear the victims of Pan would spiral down to their deaths. Yet to those who deliberately ventured toward Pan and chose to pay him worship, he was harmless. He bestowed upon his willing visitors abundance, health, and the ultimate gift—wisdom. We've all got our own Pans. If we can stop avoiding and running from them—and learn to face them instead—wisdom is ours to gain.

Someone who knows this well is Sara Bareilles. Back in 2014, with four albums and multiple hits to her name, Bareilles was beginning to burn out. She decided to step away from pop celebrity and the recording scene and went back to her roots, focusing on the craft of songwriting, without the other distractions. Out of this period emerged the musical *Waitress*, for which Bareilles wrote the music and lyrics. The show opened on Broadway in the spring of 2016. It was a smashing success, earning Bareilles a Tony nomination for best original score. She often talks about how transitioning from the stressors, individual pressures, and highs and lows of the pop music industry to concentrate on writing a musical helped rekindle her love for the art of songwriting. It also gave her space to explore some of her own vulnerabilities. In 2019, Bareilles released her first post-*Waitress* studio album, which pulled no punches and cut right to the chase. The album, titled *Amidst the Chaos*, is full of songs describing how to live a full and grounded life during commotion and disorder, how to stay strong and unshakable amid so many storms. Shortly after the album was released, Bareilles told NPR that creating *Amidst the Chaos* made her more vulnerable than ever. The album pushed her writing, piano, and vocals in new and uncomfortable ways. Not to mention, many of the tracks detail her own struggles with anxiety, fear, and sadness in a way that her past work does not.

"In my heart of hearts, I don't feel like there is such a thing as too close to the darkness. I think we can't be afraid of what is, and the closer we can go to what's just true, it sort of takes the bite out of it," Bareilles told NPR. She says that the more she is "willing to share the deepest and darkest parts" of her experience, the closer she feels to her work, and the closer she feels to herself.

When we choose to visit Pan, hard as it can be, wisdom and inner strength are ours to gain.

FROM IMPOSTOR SYNDROME TO HUMILITY, GENUINE CONFIDENCE, AND STRENGTH

The stories of Kevin Love, DeMar DeRozan, and Sara Bareilles teach us that we are all perfectly imperfect, even those of us who appear rock solid and successful. We are all just doing the best we can, and in many ways making it up as we go.

In my coaching practice, I have the privilege of working with incredible individuals who are peak performers in their various professions. I often feel like I don't have all the answers. When I first started coaching, this was a significant concern of mine. I felt a sense of impostor syndrome. I can remember going to meet with clients and on the way thinking to myself, *What could I possibly teach this person? Just wait until they find me out, find out who I really am.* What I learned over time, and am still learning, is that no one has all the answers—including my clients.

If anyone says or comes across like they have everything figured out, that's generally a good sign to run in the other direction. The appearance of fervent confidence and absolute certainty may seem like signs of strength, but they are usually signs of weakness. Why? Because if someone or something disrupts your model, worldview, or sense of yourself, then you are prone to falling apart. Pushing away your vulnerabilities and trying to convince yourself and others that you are more certain than you are is one of the surest ways to develop impostor syndrome. Because deep down inside, you know you are faking it.

By knowing that you don't know everything, that you don't always have it together, you become more—not less—robust and grounded. You become stronger and more confident. Social scientists sometimes refer to this paradox as *intellectual humility*, which can be understood as confidence gained by owning one's limitations and not being overly concerned with being the best or having power over others. It involves active curiosity about your blind spots and perceived weaknesses. Intellectual humility is associated with greater self-awareness, discernment, and openness to new ideas. When you start from a place of humility you end up gaining a stronger, more flexible, and more integrated sense of self.

When you are vulnerable and humble, you not only become more confident and connected to yourself, but you become more connected to others, too. When Kevin Love and DeMar DeRozan put down the weight of heroic individualism and shared their stories of panic, anxiety, and depression, they received thousands of supportive letters from fans and admirers around the world. Other NBA players began to share their own struggles and an entire mental health movement within the NBA emerged. The league began to run nationally televised commercials on the importance of addressing mental health challenges, and implemented new guidelines mandating that every NBA organization have a mental health professional on staff.

When Sara Bareilles poured her soul into *Amidst the Chaos*, she won her first Grammy, for a song called "Saint Honesty," a particularly revealing track. It's not surprising that this song resonated with so many listeners. In her memoir, *Sounds Like Me*, Bareilles writes that over time she's learned, "Sharing the truth of my own pain and vulnerability could also create a vehicle for connection with others."

The resounding theme is clear. When we open up with others about our vulnerabilities, we may at first feel weak, lonely, and isolated. Ultimately, however, we gain further strength, confidence, and connection.

FORGING TRUST WITH OTHERS

Often, holding your vulnerabilities alone can feel like too much, and for good reason. It can genuinely *be* too much. The human species is fragile and flawed. From the day we come out of the womb to the day we die, we are caught in the uncomfortable tension of being a discrete individual and yet yearning to be loved, connected, and held in something beyond ourselves. We want to be both separate and together at the same time, and we need all the help we can get. Perhaps this is why we evolved to share our vulnerabilities with other members of our tribe.

Consider the "vulnerable ape" hypothesis, which goes like this: Many millennia ago, the evolutionary process shifted from selecting for traits like brute strength to selecting for traits like vulnerability, compassion, and connection. Our ancestors who survived weren't those who were the strongest by traditional measures, but those who were most effectively able to share their weaknesses with one another and work together to overcome them. It is believed that these "vulnerable apes" formed the foundation for what became *Homo sapiens*, or us.

Today, the capacity for expressing vulnerability is fully hardwired and expresses itself immediately. Within just one hour of being born, human infants adjust their heads to make eye contact with their mother's gaze. On day two or three, babies start responding to their mother's voice. As helpless infants this is how we show our vulnerability and bond with our caretakers. And this is how we survive.

Vulnerability confers bonding advantages upon us in adulthood, too, remaining the connective tissue for close relationships. Researchers at the University of Mannheim, in Germany, conducted a series of seven experiments in which they had adult participants share information about themselves with one another at varying levels of vulnerability. They repeatedly found that the individual doing the sharing felt that their vulnerability would be perceived as weak, as a negative. But the person on the other end of the conversation, the listener, felt the exact opposite: the more vulnerable the sharer was, the more courageous they perceived him or her to be. The listener viewed vulnerability as an unambiguously positive trait.

"Confessing romantic feelings, asking for help, or taking responsibility for a mistake constitute just a few examples of situations that require showing one's vulnerability," write the researchers from the University of Mannheim. "Out of fear, many individuals decide against it." But this, the researchers conclude, is a mistake. "Even when examples of showing vulnerability might sometimes feel more like weakness from the inside, our findings indicate that, to others, these acts might look more like courage from the outside. Given the positive consequences [increased trust and connection, improved learning from others, and forgiveness after making a mistake] of showing vulnerability for relationship quality, health, or job performance, it might, indeed, be beneficial to try to overcome one's fears and to choose to see the beauty in the mess of vulnerable situations." The University of Mannheim researchers aptly coined their finding "the beautiful mess effect."

Deep down on the inside, most everyone dislikes pretending that they have everything together. No one does, and keeping up the act is exhausting. When you let your guard down and get real, others don't view you as weak. Rather, they are relieved. They think: *Finally, someone who isn't faking it. Someone who is more like me.* They gain the permission and confidence to stop their own tiring act of perfection and start revealing their cracks instead. As this cycle intensifies—one vulnerable offering leading to another—tight bonds of trust and connection are forged. In this way, when you are vulnerable it doesn't just remove your shackles. It removes the shackles from those around you, too. The result is more freedom and trust, which supports better, more nourishing, and more effective relationships. The irony is that all the time and energy we spend developing a personal brand and worrying about being put together is a hindrance to creating the kind of close bonds that we desire most. Long before any experimental science and "beautiful mess effect," the Taoists knew the social benefits of being vulnerable. In the fourth century BC, the Taoist philosopher Lao-tzu wrote, "When you are content to simply be yourself and don't compare or compete, everybody will respect you."

VULNERABILITY AND PERFORMANCE

The groundbreaking work of Harvard professor and researcher Amy C. Edmondson demonstrates that regardless of the field, the highest-performing teams all exemplify what she calls *psychological safety*. Psychological safety occurs when team members feel that they are able to show and deploy their whole selves without fear of negative repercussions. Edmondson's inquiry started in hospitals, where she found that the more comfortable team members were with one another, the more they spoke up when they spotted something wrong, averting potentially life-threatening errors. (Think: a nurse or medical assistant being able to question the chief surgeon.) When she extended her research into other domains, Edmondson found that psychologically safe teams get along better, overcome obstacles more efficiently, communicate more openly, and score higher on common indicators of quality in their respective fields. Psychological safety develops when individuals on a team have mutual respect and trust for one another. As you might guess, vulnerability is perhaps the most fundamental driver of both. "All of us are vulnerable," she says. "The decision is whether to admit it or not. Recommendation? Acknowledging your humanness creates a safe place for others to bring their selves forward."

Vulnerability doesn't come easy. This is especially true if you have been living in a guarded state, spending much of your life performing as your front stage self. It may seem easier to pretend to be someone else, but it's not. Any acute discomfort that comes from being vulnerable is outweighed by lasting gains in freedom, trust, and connection, both with yourself and with others, the result of which is increased groundedness. The following practices are meant to help you develop vulnerability. Remember, it is only by confronting and exploring your cracks that you become more solid.

PRACTICE: DEVELOP EMOTIONAL FLEXIBILITY

Throughout your day, pay attention and see if you find yourself regularly running away from certain thoughts, feelings, or situations. This can be anything from not wanting to spend time with a dying family member, to long-standing hesitancy to speak up in key meetings at the workplace, to avoiding situations where you may feel lonely. Once you've identified a few areas of avoidance, set aside some time for formal reflection and contemplation. For each difficult thought, feeling, or situation, ask yourself the following:

- What am I running from? What do I fear?

- What lies underneath this fear?

- What if this fear—be it of irrelevance, failure, losing control, running out of time, embarrassment, or death—is simply an unavoidable part of the human condition?

- What would it look like to make space for this fear, first in myself, and then perhaps by being more open about it with others?

- What lies on the other side of this fear, of this perceived weakness? What are my strengths? What do I really want? Love? Connection? Acceptance? Safety? Can I follow that true and deeply held desire? What would it be like to hold all of this—my fears, my strengths, and my true desires—at once?

- How might I use this fear and the true desires lying underneath it as a catalyst for taking productive action, or for becoming more connected to myself and potentially others?

The act of investigating your fears in this way changes your relationship to them.

Though it may be tough at first, over time you will no longer feel as strong an urge to repress them or push them away. Instead of shutting down or freezing up, you can lean into your fears and let them guide you toward what you really want. You will come to know all of yourself better, and thus you will come to gain more trust and confidence in all of yourself too.

You may also develop what psychologists call *emotional flexibility*, or the capacity to experience a wider range of emotions and more easily transition between them without losing your ground. Emotional flexibility is essential to living a considered, thoughtful, and whole life, and research shows that it is associated with enhanced performance, well-being, and general satisfaction. This isn't surprising. The human condition demands that we hold multiple emotions at once and skillfully navigate them. After all, on the other side of sadness there is happiness, on the other side of death there is life, and on the other side of loneliness there is love and connection.

PRACTICE: ASK YOURSELF WHAT YOU REALLY WANT TO SAY—AND THEN SAY THAT

I once had a coaching client named Dale who struggled with impostor syndrome. He was in a big new role at his company and felt pressure to act like he had it all together, especially when speaking in front of large groups. He became nervous and scared, and he felt all alone and isolated onstage. I asked him if he thought that I had it all together. (I promptly reminded him about my OCD, which he had read about publicly.) Then, I asked him how my vulnerabilities affected our relationship. He didn't hesitate. "I trust you much more knowing you are honest and real," he told me. "I'm more comfortable opening up to you about my own insecurities, like this one, because of it."

I proceeded to ask Dale if the same might be true for the thousands of people in his organization. Might they trust him more if they knew he was real? Might he trust himself more if he could be real? The next time he spoke to a large group, he opened by saying something along the lines of: "I'm not really sure how I got into this role and at times I feel like I am in over my head, but I'm doing the best that I can. Let me tell you about how I'm doing just that and then open myself up to all of your ideas so I—so we—can do even better." Dale and I had another session shortly after he gave this talk. He told me that he's never felt freer, more at ease, and more comfortable in his own skin while speaking to a large audience. He also noticed that his audience was more engaged and connected than ever, too.

If you catch yourself pretending or performing, exerting too much effort to maintain your front stage self, use that feeling of pretending as a cue to pause and ask yourself what you really want to say. Then, so long as it is not harmful or hurtful, say that—or at least something closer to that. You can use this approach in a variety of situations, be it a family dinner, a small meeting, or speaking in front of thousands of people. As with many of the practices in this book, you may find this challenging at first, especially when the rubber meets the road, in the moment you need to summon the courage to say what you really want to say. You can always increase your vulnerability progressively, starting small and gradually exposing more of your backstage self over time. As you do, you should begin to feel stronger and more confident. And you should start to realize that it is easier to genuinely connect with others, too.

PRACTICE: REMIND YOURSELF THAT EVERYONE IS GOING THROUGH SOMETHING

The title of the NBA star Kevin Love's essay in which he opens up about his panic and anxiety is "Everyone Is Going Through Something." DeMar DeRozan says that his mom always told him, "Never make fun of anybody because you never know what that person is going through. . . . You never know." Love and DeRozan are right, and I am so glad they are sharing this message from their large platforms. According to the research profiled in this chapter, most people are just waiting for an opportunity to open up about what they are going through. Sharing our vulnerabilities with others is a lot easier than holding them alone. Merely verbalizing a challenging thought, feeling, or situation to another person has a powerful way of taking the edge off, making whatever it is you are going through easier, even if only a little, to work with.

If you feel like you are all alone, remind yourself that you are not. Give others the chance to be vulnerable by being vulnerable yourself. Remember that vulnerability doesn't come from trust—trust comes from vulnerability. If you attempt to open up to someone and it is not well received, don't take it personally. Move on to others who will meet you where you are. If being vulnerable in person feels like too much, start with a phone call, text message, email, or handwritten letter. If you are not receiving support from those in your community, or if you find your vulnerabilities overwhelming, consider working with a skilled therapist or coach. No one is better equipped for these kinds of conversations.

FINAL THOUGHTS ON VULNERABILITY

Vulnerability means leaning into our soft spots, perceived weaknesses, and the things that we fear most. Vulnerability is hard work, which explains why we put up walls around our hearts and harden our souls. Though we may think this makes us stronger, we are mistaken. It actually makes us weaker; it makes us fragile. When we do not fully know ourselves we cannot fully trust ourselves. And when we cannot fully trust ourselves, we cannot be strong, confident, and grounded, at least not in a genuine manner.

Vulnerability also builds trust with others, but only if it is authentic and raw, not performative. This isn't about sharing that your biggest weakness is that you try too hard at your job or that you sometimes stay up too late at night. It's about sharing that you've experienced depression. That you've lost a child. That you've been through a divorce. That you've failed at projects you care deeply about. That you're scared about getting sick. That you're scared to die.

There is, of course, a time and a place to share these vulnerabilities. It's probably not the first time you meet someone, or your first week at a new job. But far more often than not, people lean away from appropriate expressions of vulnerability when it would be beneficial to lean into them. Life is too short to go around pretending. The more real you can get with both yourself and others, even if you do so gradually, the better. On the other side of these insecurities and fears lie not only trust, strength, and confidence but also love and connection.

Vulnerability is a conduit to community, and community holds vulnerability. Community also sustains acceptance, presence, and patience. It is the supportive space in which a grounded life unfolds, through ups and downs. It is the principle of groundedness we'll turn to next.

6

BUILD DEEP COMMUNITY

The old-growth redwoods in Felton, California, are awesome. These trees tower two hundred feet above the ground, with trunks that can span more than ten feet in diameter. What's fascinating is that the roots that support these massive redwoods run only six to twelve feet deep. Instead of growing downward, they grow outward, extending hundreds of feet laterally, wrapping themselves around the roots of their neighbors. When rough weather comes, it is this expansive network of closely intertwined roots that supports the trees' ability to stand strong as individuals. There is much we can learn from the redwoods. We, too, are meant to be part of a network that is larger than us. We, too, thrive in collectives. We, too, are most grounded when we are enmeshed in tightly knit communities.

I learned this lesson firsthand when I was in my twenties,

beginning to write professionally and spending most of my time working from home. Though I was happy to be doing work I loved, I noticed, somewhere between my chest and my gut, a sensation of something being not quite right, of something missing. I felt lonely. At the time, this didn't make sense. Thanks to the proliferation of digital technology, it was easier and cheaper than ever to reach out to family, friends, and colleagues pretty much anywhere and at any time. I regularly Facebook-messaged with a friend who lives in the mountain regions of Nepal; used Twitter to discuss the topics I write about with experts all over the world; participated in an ongoing group email with friends whom I love and admire; and texted family members while walking to my favorite coffee shop. Many of the people who were most important to me were at my fingertips. By all accounts, or so I thought, I was more connected than ever. Yet at times I still felt this sense of being alone. I didn't feel down or dramatically off. But I didn't feel quite right, either.

Unfortunately, this feeling is commonplace. Research of the late John T. Cacioppo, a psychologist who pioneered the scientific study of loneliness and directed the Center for Cognitive and So-cial Neuroscience at the University of Chicago, shows that the rate of loneliness in America has more than tripled in the past few de-cades, up from 11 percent in the 1980s to around 40 percent in 2010. Other research, conducted by AARP and the Harris Poll, puts this number at between 30 and 35 percent for regular loneli-ness and as high as 72 percent for occasional loneliness. A poll conducted in 2018 by the health insurer Cigna found that 50 per-cent of Americans report feeling lonely.

Loneliness is a subjective feeling. An introverted person may not need the same level of social interaction to feel good as someone who is extroverted. For this reason, Cacioppo and other experts define loneliness broadly, as a desire for connections that you do not have. The great paradox, of course, is that rates of loneliness are skyrocketing at a time when we are more connected, at least digitally, than ever—a theme we'll explore later in this chapter. But first, let's briefly review why growing rates of loneliness are so worrisome.

Loneliness is associated with elevated levels of the stress hormone cortisol, poor sleep quality, an increased risk for heart disease and stroke, accelerated cognitive decline, heightened systemic inflammation, reduced immune function, anxiety, and depression. Researchers from Brigham Young University put all of this together for a comprehensive study that followed more than 300,000 people for an average of 7.5 years. They learned that the mortality risks associated with loneliness exceed those associated with obesity and physical inactivity and are comparable to those associated with smoking.

The deleterious effects of loneliness extend beyond our individual experience and into our romantic partnerships, too. Relationship therapist Esther Perel believes that a driving issue in many unsatisfying intimate relationships is that participants lack belonging to a broader community. "We are asking one person to give us what once an entire village of people used to provide," she says. "It's crushing us. It puts way too many expectations [on the relationship]." Yes, humans evolved to bond with intimate others, but we also evolved to belong to communities. Our ability to survive, let alone thrive, relies upon being members of a tribe. Asking ourselves or just one other person to fulfill all of our needs is impractical and unwise.

The fifth principle of groundedness is *deep community*. Heroic individualism's incessant drive to be "productive," "optimized," and "efficient" often crowds out time and energy otherwise spent forging close bonds, both to other people and to traditions, crafts, and lineages that provide a sense of belonging. The irony is that these close bonds not only make us feel better and make the world a better place, but they help us perform better, too.

DEEP COMMUNITY IS A BASIC HUMAN NEED

In researching his groundbreaking book, *Tribe*, investigative reporter Sebastian Junger found that many soldiers are more satisfied at war than at home. Though on its face this may seem perplexing, Junger learned that while at war soldiers feel a much stronger sense of belonging. "Humans don't mind hardship, in fact they thrive on it," he writes. "What they mind is not feeling necessary. Modern society has perfected the art of making people not feel necessary."

Junger's observation of soldiers aligns with decades of research conducted on the fundamental elements that drive human motivation, satisfaction, and fulfillment. This body of work has coalesced into *self-determination theory*, or SDT for short. SDT demonstrates that humans thrive when three basic needs are met:

1. *Autonomy*, or the ability to have at least some control over how we spend our time and energy.

3. *Competence*, or a path toward tangible improvement in our chosen pursuits.

4. *Relatedness*, or a sense of connection and belonging.

When one or more of these basic needs go unmet, health and well-being deteriorate and rates of burnout increase. No matter how much we think we can go it alone, the research shows we can't—at least not well or sustainably.

We are social animals. Our ability to communicate and cooperate has been one of our species' greatest competitive advantages. Millennia ago, back on the savanna, groups of primates and early humans who were tightly bonded had a significant edge over groups who were not. Consequently, over time, evolution favored well-functioning groups, as well as individuals who had a knack for participating in these groups. Scientists refer to this process as *group selection*.

The evolutionary psychologist Jonathan Haidt believes that group selection is how we developed what he calls our "social instincts." For example, an early human going it alone would be far more likely to get picked off by a predator or starve during a time of famine. But not so for someone in a group with members who protect each other, comfort each other, and share resources.

Even today, research shows that belonging to a community comes with strong advantages for our primate ancestors. A 2003 study out of the University of California, Los Angeles, found that a female baboon's level of social integration and belonging could predict the chances that her infants would survive. Later research, published between 2010 and 2014, found that tight social bonds didn't extend life just for the infants, but for their mothers, too. Baboons who were socially isolated, meanwhile, experienced a greater rate of illness and often showed behaviors that look similar to human distress.

When you put all of this together it becomes clear that community and belonging are not "nice to haves" or ancillary elements of our existence. Rather, they are central to our essence, to our ability to be well and thrive. It is in our DNA.

Writing in his 1941 book, *Escape from Freedom*, the psychologist, sociologist, and philosopher Erich Fromm explained, "To feel completely alone and isolated leads to mental disintegration just as physical starvation leads to death." However, he writes that while relatedness is often physical, it need not always be. "Relatedness to others is not identical with physical contact. An individual may be alone in a physical sense for many years and yet he may be related to ideas, values, or at least social patterns that give him a feeling of communion and 'belonging.' On the other hand, he may live among people and yet be overcome with an utter feeling of isolation." The remainder of this chapter argues that we are most satisfied when we fulfill both of these essential drives: <u>an inner feeling of belonging and appropriate outward contact with other people.</u> It argues that these two drives, which taken together I call *deep community*, complement and strengthen one another, resulting in a more profound and resolute groundedness.

LONELINESS AND COMMUNITY
BUILD ON THEMSELVES

John Cacioppo's research shows that when you are connected to others you not only feel good but you also feel secure. Likewise, you don't just feel bad when you are isolated, but you also feel insecure. While you may not actually be physically threatened when you are alone, your mind-body system, programmed by millennia of evolution, starts to fire warning signals. This is precisely why loneliness is associated with elevated stress hormones, high blood pressure, and poor sleep quality. In many ways, loneliness can look a lot like anxiety.

The physiological feelings of discomfort that accompany loneliness serve the same purpose today as they did thousands of years ago. They are an instinctual signal to connect. In modern times this means picking up the phone and calling a friend, making social arrangements, or at the very least leaving the house and going into a public space. If someone becomes chronically lonely, however, those same feelings of distress can compound and have the opposite effect, encouraging people to shut down and further isolate themselves.

Here's how this works. When you start to experience chronic loneliness, your baseline perception of threat increases. Think back to evolution: if you didn't have a group surrounding you, the pressure to stay safe and secure would fall solely on your shoulders. You'd constantly be scanning for danger, perhaps even forgoing sleep. Unfortunately, someone who feels constantly under threat and is worried about themselves has a harder time being empathetic toward and connecting with others. This initiates a vicious cycle, causing even more loneliness.

To prove this, in one of his studies Cacioppo induced loneliness in college students using hypnosis. He and his colleagues took participants back to periods of their lives when they experienced both loneliness and connection. They then administered tests of social skills. They found that once the students were made to feel lonely, they scored much lower on the tests, an effect that was present for even the most outgoing students. Rather than looking for connection, the students who were hypnotized to feel lonely were too busy scanning their environment, both internal and external, for signs of threat. When participants were made to feel well connected, however, they performed strongly on tests of social ability.

In an effort to trace the neurological correlates for this behavior, Cacioppo used fMRI technology to look under the hood of lonely people versus non-lonely people. The brains of the lonely people activated much more quickly when confronted with negative cues, and they were more likely to rate neutral cues as dangerous. In other words, the brains of lonely people were continually scanning for threats and primed to identify them; in essence, they were always on edge. This is not a great state of mind for making connections.

Fortunately, there is reason to believe the opposite effect is also true. Much like loneliness builds upon itself, so, too, does community. As you meet and authentically connect with a greater number of people, you expand your social skills and confidence. You go from feeling lonely and threatened to feeling part of the group. The more community you gain the more secure you feel. Instead of being preoccupied with worrying about yourself, you free up capacity to reach out to others—bonding with additional friends, then friends of friends, and so on.

Long before today's heroic individualism and ensuing loneliness epidemic, ancient wisdom noted the importance of deep community. In book eight of his *Confessions*, the fourth-century Christian theologian Saint Augustine describes his conversion not only as a pathway to a more spiritual life but also as a commitment to a community of people whom he needs and loves. Though many associate Saint Augustine's spirituality with inner strength and individualism, to him, a self is strong only insofar as it is situated in a community. Throughout his life, he would remark, "I could not be happy without friends." Friendship gave Saint Augustine's life meaning. In a famous sermon delivered sometime in the fourth century, he remarked that "in this world two things are essential: a healthy life and friendship."

Prior to that and eastward, the earliest Buddhist teachings explained that there are three jewels, three fundamental aspects of life that are important to prioritize always: the Buddha, which represents the deep internal awareness in all of us; the dharma, or the teachings of the spiritual path; and the sangha, or the community you are to build along the way.

In a passage appearing in the Pali Canon, one of the oldest remaining Buddhist texts, the Buddha's loyal attendant, Ananda, approaches the Buddha and asks, "Venerable sir, this is half of the spiritual life, that is, good friendship, good companionship, good comradeship."

The Buddha replies enthusiastically yet sternly: "Not so,

Ananda! Not so! This is the entire spiritual life, that is good friendship, good companionship, good comradeship."

TECHNOLOGY AND DEEP COMMUNITY

A recurring theme throughout this book is how digital technology has infiltrated our lives. It seems unlikely that there is any turning back. When it comes to community in particular, digital technology presents two interrelated dilemmas:

1. *Digital technology has created the ability—and ensuing pressure—for us to "optimize" and be productive always, which often comes at the expense of time and energy spent building deep community.* In their book, *The Lonely American: Drifting Apart in the Twenty-first Century*, Harvard psychiatry professors Jacqueline Olds and Richard Schwartz profile the rise of loneliness and the decline of meaningful relationships. One of the driving forces, they write, is an increased focus on "productivity and the cult of busyness." Olds and Schwartz explain that too much tunnel vision and time spent on work has led to a sharp decline in deep communities and a subsequent rise in social isolation and related mood disorders.

The research of Olds and Schwartz brings to mind writing of the poet-philosopher David Whyte. In his book *Crossing the Unknown Sea: Work as a Pilgrimage of Identity*, which was published in 2001, before we all had smartphones in our pockets, Whyte warns about the stark dangers of neglecting community when work becomes all-consuming. "The dynamic of friendship is almost always underestimated as a constant force in human life," he writes. "A diminishing circle of friends is the first terrible diagnostic of a life in deep trouble: of overwork, of too much emphasis on a professional identity, of forgetting who will be there when our armored personalities run into the inevitable natural disasters and vulnerabilities found in even the most average existence."

Long before that, in his 1897 groundbreaking work *Suicide*, the French sociologist Émile Durkheim observed that "Society cannot disintegrate without the individual detaching himself from social life, without his own goals becoming preponderant over those of the community, in a word without his personality tending to surmount the collective personality. The more weakened the groups to which he belongs, the less he depends on them, the more he consequently depends only on himself and recognizes no other rules of conduct than what are founded on his private interests. If we agree to call this state egoism, in which the individual ego asserts itself to excess in the face of social ego and at its expense," Durkheim goes on, "we may call . . . [this a] special type of suicide springing from excessive individualism." I can only imagine what Durkheim would have to say about today's heroic individualism, its consequences, and the importance of groundedness as an alternative.

2. *Many digital technologies offer us the illusion of connection while eroding the real thing.* We think that if we can tweet, post, text, direct-message, or email someone, then we're making a connection, and we're doing it in an *efficient* manner. But this is wishful thinking. As you'll see in the coming pages, while effective in certain situations, digital connection cannot replace the power of real-life interaction.

Many of us fall prey to these two interrelated problems. It is the nature of heroic individualism that we face increasing pressure and insecurity about not being online always. And we possess super-powered computers in our homes and even our pockets. The result is that we work constantly, and in doing so we have less time and energy for community building. Sometimes it gets crowded out in such subtle ways that we don't even realize. Here are a few personal examples, none of which are problematic in and of themselves, but all of which are problematic when they become habitual, which they all too easily do:*

- I've frequently found myself tempted to go to the gym alone instead of with workout buddies. Though I know the latter makes me feel better, the former ensures I can go on my own schedule and as efficiently as possible, causing less of an interruption in my ability to get more work done.

- I've often opted to stay in my apartment to work rather than head to the coffee shop because I was concerned about interrupting my writing groove or wasting time commuting.

- I've gotten sucked into social media when I could have phoned a close friend or gone out and done something meaningful (in person) with other people.

---

*All of these examples assume it is safe to carry on with these sorts of activities. As of this writing, much of the world is still deep in the throes of the COVID-19 pandemic. That said, eventually this pandemic will pass. It will likely leave in its wake increased inertia of not gathering in person even when it is safe—and arguably more important than ever—to do so.

This last example is a particularly interesting one, given the relative novelty and ubiquity of social media. It deserves further exploration.

DIGITAL CONNECTION VS. THE REAL THING

The Pew Research Center, a nonpartisan polling organization and think tank, first started tracking social media use in 2005. At the time, about 5 percent of Americans were active on social media. In 2020, that number is close to 70 percent, and most indications are that it will continue to rise. Whether you like it or not, social media is a significant facet of modern life. In recent years, it has been in vogue to bash social media for destroying all that is good, including community. But the truth is more complicated. Writing in her 2020 book, *Friendship: The Evolution, Biology, and Extraordinary Power of Life's Fundamental Bond*, author and social science researcher Lydia Denworth explains that when it comes to studies on social media and community, "the results to date have been so mixed that they amount to a scientific version of he said, she said. For every study that finds a rise in loneliness with social media use, there is another one showing an increase in connection."

Consider a few examples: For a comprehensive meta-analysis, the psychologist Jeff Hancock, who runs the Social Media Lab at Stanford University, combined data from 226 papers published between 2006 and 2018. In total, these studies included more than 275,000 people. He wanted to answer once and for all the question of whether social media is positive or negative for community and connection. The result? It depends. Hancock found <u>that social media yields a mix of benefits and costs</u>. Overall, the effect of social media on relationships was not notable in either direction. "Using social media is essentially a tradeoff," he says. "You get very small advantages for your well-being that come with very small costs."

Hancock's results track with another comprehensive research project, published in 2019, this one conducted by Andrew Przybylski and Amy Orben from the University of Oxford. They reviewed data on more than 350,000 adolescents and found that social media use has almost no effect on their well-being. Around the time their results were published Przybylski and Orben made headlines in many major magazines for pointing out that the association between social media use and adolescent well-being is about equivalent to the association between well-being and "eating potatoes."

However, a study conducted at the University of Pittsburgh came to a different conclusion. There, researchers examined a nationally representative sample of two thousand people and found that increased social media use—in terms of both frequency of visits to social media sites as well as the duration of each visit—was correlated with higher perceived loneliness.

At the time this book is being published, social media is still in its infancy, at least in scientific terms. As the years pass, additional research will help us learn more about its short-term and long-term effects. For now, experts believe that the mixed results of research studies represent an important nuance when it comes to social media. If you use social media to augment in-person community—to meet people online and then get together off-line; to find groups of people with similar interests; to stay in touch with those in other geographies or when you cannot meet in person—then it can be beneficial. If you use social media as a substitute for in-person community and other, richer forms of connection, however, it can be deleterious.* As far as we know, nothing can replace in-person connection. Studies show that <u>presence and physical touch are critical for empathy, connection</u>, and <u>belonging</u>. Anyone who has ever been in a tough situation and been comforted by someone putting a hand on their shoulder or making empathetic eye contact knows this firsthand.[†]

"If you use those [digital] connections as a way station—kids tend to do this; they use Facebook so that they can then meet up somewhere—it's associated with lower levels of loneliness," says Cacioppo. "If it's used as a *destination*," he says, not so much. "Ironically, lonely people tend to do this, they tend to withdraw socially because it's punishing, and interacting digitally, perhaps as a non-authentic self, makes them feel more like they're accepted. But it doesn't actually make them feel less lonely."

Another important caveat to the research mentioned here is that it only examines social media's effect on forging community. More and more, we are seeing how social media can have a destructive effect on democracy via the dissemination of conspiracy theories and other fake news. We are also seeing how it can lead to increased

---

*Additionally, digital connection can be beneficial when you simply cannot get together with others in person. For example, during the COVID-19 pandemic of 2020, much of the world was under shelter-in-place orders, and people were prohibited from gathering with others outside of their family units. During this challenging period, digital tools for connection served as the best option to support each other and sustain community. Even then, it certainly seemed that the closer to in-person connection the technolovgy was, the better. A phone call was more beneficial than a text message, a video chat was more beneficial than a phone call, and a socially distanced outdoor meetup was more beneficial than a video chat.

†This is precisely what made COVID-19 so hard for so many people. At a time when we needed in-person support and connection more than ever, it wasn't safe to have it. In order to stop the spread of the virus, we had to refrain from the most instinctual thing to do during challenging times: putting our hands on each other's shoulders.

political tribalism, particularly when it's used as a place to anonymously exchange ideas (at best) and attack others (at worst, and sadly far more often), not as a way station to facilitate thoughtful real-life gatherings of people with opposing views (where differences can be discussed with less vitriol). Additionally, if you are using social media as a way to incessantly compare yourself to others; seek validation in the way of retweets, Likes, or comments; or stay abreast of every so-called breaking news story, then it is probably not promoting lasting satisfaction or well-being. Social media also becomes problematic if you struggle to turn it off. For example, research shows that babies do not bond as well with their parents if their parents are constantly on their phones. And if you are on your phone when meeting up with other people in person, regardless of age, the quality of those interactions deteriorates significantly.

While social media may not be inherently bad, you should understand its pitfalls, use it only as a tool, and with the utmost caution. Something I've noticed recently is people who have massive online communities and boast tons of friends, followers, and Likes on platforms such as Facebook, Twitter, Instagram, LinkedIn, and TikTok. These people tend to be beacons of heroic individualism, on top of everything always, devastatingly put together. Yet it seems these very same people are often desperately wanting for deeper connection in their lives. This is likely the case for many of the reasons I've discussed, including because they spend so much time and energy on their online communities that they have none left to invest in their actual community; they lack the comfort of physical touch and connection; and in some cases, they spend too much time swimming in the cesspool of angry forums and feeds. "If the only acceptance you can get of yourself is a fake representation on the web, that's not going to make you feel connected," says Cacioppo.

Decades before social media and Cacioppo's studies on its deleterious effects, Erich Fromm, in his 1955 book *The Sane Society*, warned against developing a *marketing orientation*: "[When someone's] body, mind, and soul are his capital, and his task in life is to invest it favorably, to make a profit of himself. Human qualities like friendliness, courtesy, kindness, are transformed into commodities, into assets of the 'personality package,' conducive to a higher price on the personality market. If the individual fails in a profitable investment of himself, he feels that *he* is a failure; if he succeeds, *he* is a success." A marketing orientation certainly sounds isolating and depressing. Yet more than ever, enabled by the worst of social media, so many people are selling their souls for a shot at internet stardom. But to what end?

Remember, more than seventy thousand years of evolution have programmed us not for digital connection and belonging but for the real thing. As far as I can tell, it is exponentially more fulfilling to be deeply involved, to be a celebrity in your local community rather than a celebrity on the internet, as addictive as the latter can be.

THE PEOPLE WITH WHOM YOU SURROUND YOURSELF SHAPE YOU

Like the massive redwood trees with which I opened this chapter, when we ground ourselves in community we become deeply intertwined with it. Studies reveal that if you bear witness to someone else experiencing pain—whether it's a friend stubbing their toe on a bookcase, a person experiencing homelessness on a damp street corner, or a somber face in the waiting room of a hospital—you're likely to experience some degree of pain yourself. The Association for Psychological Science (APS) dubs this the "I feel your pain" effect, and most everyone experiences it from time to time. The closer your bond to the person in pain, the stronger the effect. This, too, is part of our evolutionary programming, prompting us to help others in our group when they are in need.

"When we witness what happens to others, we don't just activate the visual cortex like we thought some decades ago," Dutch neuroscientist Christian Keysers told the APS. "We also activate our own actions as if we'd be acting in similar ways. We activate our own emotions and sensations as if we felt the same."

Pain isn't the only contagious emotion. Researchers from Yale University closely monitored nearly five thousand people living in the small town of Framingham, Massachusetts, for more than three decades. They found that when someone became happy or sad, that emotion rippled throughout the entire town. Emotions even spread virtually. Another study, aptly titled "I'm Sad You're Sad," found that if you are in a negative mood when you text-message your partner, they are likely to pick up on it and experience a lower mood state themselves. The same is true of Facebook posts, according to research published in the *Proceedings of the National Academy of Sciences*. Emotions like happiness, sadness, and anger spread like wildfire on the platform. (Not that you needed a study to prove this.)

Another study, published in the journal *Motivation and Emo-*

tion, showed that even below-the-surface emotions, such as motivation, are contagious. If someone is working in the same room as others who are internally driven, that person's attitude improves. If, however, someone is working in the same room with those who aren't too excited about their work, then that person's motivation decreases. A 2017 study out of Northwestern University found that sitting within twenty-five feet of a high performer at work improved an employee's performance by 15 percent. But sitting within twenty-five feet of a low performer hurt their performance by 30 percent. That's an enormous impact.

Someone who knows about the strong influence of deep community on performance and well-being is my close friend Shalane Flanagan, the United States' best-ever distance runner.* When Flanagan decided that instead of training alone she'd start training in a group, her performance, along with that of all the other women in the group, soared. Every single one of her training partners— eleven women in total—has made it to the Olympics while training with her, an astonishing achievement. Lindsay Crouse, writing for *The New York Times*, coined this the "Shalane Flanagan Effect: You serve as a rocket booster for the careers of [those] who work alongside you, while catapulting forward yourself."

Not only did Flanagan and everyone else run better, but they felt better, too. Emily Infeld, an elite US distance runner, told the *Times* that shortly after she graduated college, she struggled with stress fractures and contemplated quitting the sport in 2014. That

---

*I may be biased because of our friendship, but the numbers speak for themselves. Flanagan has appeared on four Olympic teams, winning a silver medal at the 2008 games. She also won the New York City Marathon in 2017, becoming the first American woman to do so in forty years.

December, Flanagan took her aside for a glass of wine and a talk. "I was really struggling—I cried and told her 'I can't do it, my body isn't built for this,'" Infeld recalled. "And she totally changed my mind-set. She told me that of course this was bad, but she believed I could do better. I got better, we trained together and she held me accountable. It's completely changed my career." Within a matter of months, in August 2015, Infeld medaled in the ten thousand meters at the IAAF World Championships.

Flanagan benefited as much from the Shalane Flanagan Effect as anyone. "Even in such a grueling individual sport, I realized that I could feel grounded in community," she told me. "If you're lonely at the top, you're doing it wrong. High performers focus on pulling others up. They are generous as they rise and create a tribe." It is not surprising that upon her retirement from professional running at the end of 2019, Flanagan wasted little time announcing that she'd be staying in the sport to coach. The two of us talked often as she was making this decision. "These are my people," she told me. "This community gives my life so much meaning. I can't imagine doing anything else right now."

The science and experiences of highly fulfilled peak performers like Shalane Flanagan all coalesce around the same basic truth. We are mirrors reflecting one another. The people with whom we surround ourselves shape us, and we shape those around us, too. The implications are important and actionable.

For starters, we'd be wise to associate with people whom we admire and aspire to emulate. It's not so much rote skill that is contagious as it is motivation, emotion, and values. Being aware of how easily emotions spread allows you to transform yourself and, in turn, transform those around you. For example, if you receive a text message that suddenly makes you sad, or if you read a social-media post that makes you angry, rather than immediately reacting, you can pause for a moment and then respond thoughtfully. Instead of meeting sadness with sadness, you can meet it with compassion and support. Instead of meeting anger with anger, you can meet it with understanding (or just ignore it altogether, a vastly underused strategy). The flip side is also true. When you are feeling good you're liable to spread it—though my hunch is that this generally happens naturally, without trying.

These insights are long-standing. More than a decade ago on an expedition in the foothills of the Khumbu region in the Himalayas, I asked a Nepali Sherpa named Indra about the prayer flags that were scattered all over. "It's simple," he told me. "When you are feeling a strong emotion, you plant a flag. Since the beginning of time, my culture [Tibetan Buddhism] believes that the wind will spread that energy and the universe will receive it."

PRACTICE: GET INVOLVED WITH A MEANINGFUL GROUP

One of Cacioppo's first principles for countering loneliness and building community is to seek collectives. We tend to like people who are like us, those with whom we share interests, activities, and values. There is also less pressure to hit it off when getting involved in a group versus trying to meet people one-on-one. One benefit of the internet is that it's easier than ever to find and join meaningful groups, many of which meet in real life. Here are a few particularly powerful examples.

Volunteer

When people are doing something for someone else, they tend to have an easier time overcoming their fears and insecurities, and also forging connections. When helping others, the part of your brain that would normally put on the brakes to protect your ego—your literal self—tends to relax, allowing you to take constructive risks and work through self-doubts. The research of UCLA psychology professor Shelley Taylor shows that during experiences of subjective distress, fight-or-flight isn't the only response. We also have the capacity for what she calls a tend-and-befriend response. "Tending to others is as natural, as biologically based, as searching for food or sleeping, and its origins lie deep in our social nature," writes Taylor in her book, *The Tending Instinct*. When we tend to others, we also tend to befriend those around us.

Volunteering benefits not only your community and the individuals you are helping but also you. Studies show that volunteering is associated with better physical health, mental health, and longevity. Though it is hard to pinpoint the exact mechanism underlying these positive effects, they are likely related to the broader benefits of engaging in community and connection. Volunteering may be especially powerful for individuals approaching retirement or who are recently retired. At this stage in life, we are susceptible to losing a core part of our identity, our workplace community, and how we spend our time. Volunteering helps to fill those gaps. This is precisely why the American Association of Retired Persons

(AARP) has invested in a program called Create the Good, which helps match recently retired individuals with volunteer organizations in their local communities.

Join a Faith-Based Community

Organized religion is on the decline in the United States, especially for younger people. The 2018 American Family Survey, conducted by the *Deseret News* in Utah, found that for Millennials and Gen Xers, the most common religion is no religion at all. This may not be problematic in itself, but for centuries, religion served as a driving force of community—and nothing has adequately filled its gap. A 2016 study published in *JAMA Internal Medicine* followed 75,000 women for 10 years and found that those who attended religious services at least once a week had a 33 percent lower chance of dying during the study period than their peers who did not regularly attend religious services. A 2017 study published in the journal *PLOS One* followed 5,550 adults for eighteen years and found a 55 percent reduction in mortality for those who regularly attended community religious services. The authors of these studies suspect a large part of the health and longevity benefits owes itself to the communal aspect of worship. These studies explored a diverse array of religious services. In other words, it's not that any specific belief system or deity is saving you. It's far more likely that you and the people in your community are saving each other. Remember the Buddha's advice to his loyal attendant Ananda: "Good friendship, good companionship, good comradeship is not half the spiritual life. It is the entire spiritual life." The Buddha was right.

Other research shows that the human brain evolved to be moved by singing, chanting, dancing, and other expressions of the ineffable for the sole purpose of bringing otherwise unique individuals together. Peter Sterling, professor of neuroscience at the University of Pennsylvania, calls these *sacred practices*. A species designed "where all must cooperate leads to every imaginable sort of interpersonal conflict: greed, paranoia—name it! Therefore, the design requires additional innate behaviors to dissipate psychological tensions and preserve social cohesion. Such behaviors might collectively be termed *sacred practices*, where 'sacred' means 'reverence for the ineffable'—what casual speech cannot express," he says. Given that evolution only selects for qualities that are central to a species' survival, our ability to bond over spiritual—or what Sterling calls sacred—practices is an important one.

If you've got an itch to join a faith-based community, regardless of how you were raised, don't be afraid to scratch it. It's a wonderful way to meet people with similar values. And, if like a prior version of me, you thought that there was no room for spirituality in your scientific and rational worldview, hopefully reading this book has helped you realize that spiritual wisdom and science need not oppose each other. They can actually be quite complementary. And remember that spirituality can be as simple—and as beautiful—as gathering with friends to watch the sunset, in awe of the expansive universe that we wondrously inhabit, no dogma necessary.

Join a Support Group

From mental health to studying to fitness to parenting, it's easy to use the internet to search for and find support groups for just about anything. As discussed in the previous chapter, research shows that the strength of interpersonal bonds increases with vulnerability. When you join a support group, you can more easily let go of the need to play a front stage, performative self and cut to the real stuff, since everyone "gets it," whatever "it" may be.

In addition to being a wonderful source of community, support groups also help you to overcome challenges and achieve your goals. It's not just motivation that is bolstered by community but also accountability. If you've made a commitment to another person or group, you're more likely to stick with it. If everyone shows up at the gym, the anxiety recovery group, or the Alcoholics Anonymous meeting and you don't, you'll probably feel bad. Therefore, you're more likely to show up. But an even greater benefit of community is what happens when you don't show up. You might feel embarrassed or ashamed, but you'll probably receive a pat on the back and some love. That's because everyone else in your community is undergoing the same challenges and understands how hard it is. Again, they get it. You are all being vulnerable together. You are all experiencing versions of the same-but-different story.

It's a one-two punch: community keeps you from falling, and if you do, it picks you up. This is why support groups for individuals struggling with substance abuse or other addictions are so effective. There aren't too many instances when going it alone makes more sense than going it together.

Start a Salon

Throughout the Enlightenment, artists, philosophers, poets, and scientists would regularly meet up at salons, or small private gatherings that were focused on a particular topic. Though salons have since fallen out of favor, there is no reason not to bring them back. It is as simple as assembling a group of individuals with similar interests and agreeing to meet regularly, perhaps once a month. This can take the form of a book club; a journal or article club; or a mastermind group, where people in the same vocation meet to discuss their craft.

PRACTICE: PRIORITIZE QUALITY OVER QUANTITY

More than two thousand years ago, in his masterwork *The Nicomachean Ethics*, the ancient Greek philosopher Aristotle outlined three different kinds of friendship:

1. *Friendships based on utility*, or those in which one or both of the parties gain something as a result of the friendship. This is akin to the modern "networking" enterprise, or becoming friends with someone primarily because you think they can help you.

2. *Friendships based on pleasure*, or those centered around pleasant experiences. These are the people with whom you have an enjoyable and carefree time.

3. *Friendships based on virtue*, or those in which both individuals share the same values. These are bonds with people you admire and respect, with

whom you align on what you find most important
in life.

It's fascinating that, centuries ago, Aristotle offered that "many
individuals who are young or in their prime" too often pursue
friendships predominantly for utility, only to be left wanting.
Spend some time on a college campus or in the corporate workplace and it's easy to see that some things never change.

Likewise, he wrote, "Those who love because of utility love because of what is good for themselves, and those who love because
of pleasure do so because of what is pleasant to themselves." Yet
what one finds useful or pleasurable, Aristotle wrote, "is not permanent but is always changing. Thus when the reason for the
friendship is done away, the friendship is dissolved." Here, Aristotle seems to be describing what today we might refer to as the
social climber or social butterfly, the person who floats from group
to group without ever feeling firmly grounded in a meaningful
community.

While all three of Aristotle's friendships can be advantageous in
certain circumstances, only those founded in virtue—those woven
together by shared values—are enduring and truly meaningful.
"Perfect friendship is the friendship of [those] who are alike in
virtue," he wrote. "For these [individuals] wish well to each other
[in all circumstances] and thus [these friendships] are good in
themselves." Relationships based on virtue demand effort and are
hard to come by. "Great friendships can only be felt toward a few
people," Aristotle wrote. But they yield a wonderful sense of satisfaction and contentment. It is a rare blessing to connect with someone on this deeper level, to forge a bond with a kindred spirit.

Aristotle's schema is not only prescient but also practical. It is a useful exercise to ask yourself into which categories your relationships fall. It's fine to have some, perhaps even most, friendships mainly for utility and pleasure. But recognize that these types of friendships fill a different purpose and are likely to have a shorter life span than the ultimate kind of friendship—that which is founded upon shared virtue. Friendships founded upon virtue don't emerge overnight, and they require considerable energy to maintain. As Aristotle wrote, "a lack of conversation has broken many a friendship." But what you get out of these friendships generally outweighs what you put in.

It is wise to adopt Aristotle's framework for how you think about your digital relationships, too. This is particularly relevant given what we know about how emotions spread through virtual networks. Here, the logic is straightforward and simple: if people regularly annoy, upset, or troll you, you should be quick to unfollow, unfriend, mute, mark as spam, or block them, and you shouldn't feel bad about doing so.

Aristotle wasn't the only ancient wisdom thinker who would have offered this advice for our modern situation. "If you consort with someone covered in dirt you can hardly avoid getting a little grimy yourself," wrote the Stoic philosopher Epictetus in a two-thousand-year-old warning about being around assholes. Five hundred years earlier, the Buddha taught that one of the eight elements on the noble path to enlightenment is *right speech*, which involves abstaining from gossipy, hateful, rude, and reckless conversation. It's probably best to apply the principles of right speech not just in real-life town squares but in virtual ones, too.

PRACTICE: DEVELOP A "BRAINTRUST"

Ed Catmull cofounded Pixar Animation Studios and led it throughout its ascendency and ultimate acquisition by the Walt Disney Company in 2006. Catmull, who retired in 2019, is considered one of the most successful leaders in any creative industry. Key to Pixar's success is what he calls developing a _Braintrust_, or a group of people with whom you can regularly meet to help you identify problems and give you candid feedback. This Braintrust is "an enormously beneficial and efficient entity," Catmull writes in his memoir, _Creativity, Inc._ "Even in its earliest meetings, I was struck by how constructive the feedback was. Each of the participants focused on the film at hand and not on some hidden personal agenda. . . . The members saw each other as peers."

We can all benefit from a Braintrust. The deeper we get into our own big projects—be it launching a company, training for a marathon, or raising a child—the harder time we have evaluating them objectively. While pretending you are giving advice to a friend in a situation similar to yours can be helpful (see "self-distancing" in chapter 2), actually getting advice from trusted friends is perhaps even more so. "People who take on complicated creative projects become lost at some point in the process. It is the nature of things—in order to create, you must internalize and almost _become_ the project for a while," writes Catmull. While fusing with your project can be valuable, it can also lead to blind spots. Having a Braintrust helps you identify these blind spots before they cause significant problems.

In an organizational setting, the higher up the ladder you are, the more important developing a Braintrust becomes. It is lonely at the top, and having other people to work with and support you is essential. Even more important is receiving candid feedback. Out of a fear, whether perceived or actual, of upsetting their leader, subordinates often hesitate to raise concerns or provide negative feedback. The most important people in a leader's orbit are those who are comfortable doing the opposite—challenging the leader and pointing out problems before they explode.

Catmull suggests a few guiding principles for creating a Braintrust. They hold true in both professional and personal contexts:

- Include only individuals whom you trust and who you are confident can be completely honest with you—even, and perhaps especially, if that means telling you things that you don't want to hear.

- Include people who are solutions-oriented. The goal isn't just to point out problems, but to come up with solutions and a viable path forward.

- Include those who have been there before. Surround yourself with people who have experience in what you are going through. Out of this experience comes knowledge and, equally important, empathy.

FINAL THOUGHTS ON DEEP COMMUNITY

The Zen master Thich Nhat Hanh teaches that <u>we are each like a wave in water</u>. While it is easy to get caught up in the experience of being a wave—how we rise, crest, fall, and move with the tide—it is important to remember where a wave comes from and goes back to, and what a wave actually is: <u>water.</u> When we get too caught up in our own rising and falling—too hell-bent on optimization, productivity, and efficiency—we neglect the water from which we come, and the result is a quick path to loneliness and suffering. <u>When there is no water, a wave literally loses itself.</u> Our social connections and our sense of belonging—our deep community—influence everything from our physical and mental health to our performance to our life satisfaction and fulfillment. We evolved to be in community. It is what holds us as we rise and fall. When we neglect it, we do so at great cost.

Like all the other principles of groundedness, <u>deep community is an ongoing practice.</u> It takes time and effort to build and sustain. <u>Acceptance</u>, <u>presence</u>, <u>patience,</u> and <u>especially vulnerability</u> help to create and sustain deep community. In turn, deep community becomes the supportive space for all the other principles to flourish.

"In my tradition we learn that as individuals we cannot do much. That is why . . . taking refuge in the community is a very strong and important practice," says Hanh. "Without being in a [community], without being supported by a group of friends who are motivated by the same ideal and practice, we cannot go far."

7

MOVE YOUR BODY TO GROUND YOUR MIND

You may not know the name Andrea Barber, but if you grew up in the 1990s you probably know the name Kimmy Gibbler. Barber portrayed Gibbler—the eccentric, bold, and confident next-door neighbor—on the television show *Full House*. Offstage, however, Barber was anything but confident and bold. She suffered from chronic anxiety and debilitating waves of depression, which worsened in her early adulthood. Though on the outside she was somewhat of a celebrity, recognizable in public for the perky character she played on television, on the inside she spent many years struggling.

After suffering in silence for years, at age thirty-two Barber worked up the courage to seek professional help. She was prescribed medications and began seeing a therapist regularly. Barber and I connected after I wrote the essay about my own experience with OCD. We had a lot in common: the experience of bad anxiety; working with a therapist; taking medication, even though we both still kind of stigmatized it ourselves (which just goes to show how powerful stigma can be); and having a public persona (mine significantly smaller than hers) that was, for a period of time, different from our inner experience. But more than any of that, Barber was thrilled the essay ran in *Outside* and wanted to talk to me about the power of movement.

"Running came at a time when everything in my life was in flux," she told me. "In addition to my underlying anxiety, I was also going through a separation. My emotions were all over the place. I felt like I was kind of floating. Running started as a social thing, as a way to force myself to get out in the world and be with friends. But once I got into it the more it became about getting out there and running every day. I don't know how to put it into words. It's not just about being alone with my thoughts, but also the physical movement and the rhythm of finding your cadence and your pace. I would come home from a run and feel like life wasn't as bad and all over the place as it was forty-five minutes ago before I started running."

Eventually, in 2016, Barber signed up for a marathon. It was a big goal, especially for someone new to the sport with little athletic background. But she quickly realized that it wasn't about the race (though she went on to finish it). It was about the training—the structure, consistency, and accountability it gave her to move her body every day. "It saved me," she says. "I'm convinced. Running saved me."

Though at the time of our conversations in 2020 Barber was not currently running with a particular goal in mind, she still found it essential to do something active every day. Even a brisk-paced thirty-minute walk does wonders, she says. When I asked if she thought it was simply the routine of doing the same thing every day that was helpful, she strongly disagreed. "No. I have all kinds of other routines. But none are as satisfying as physical movement. There is something special about movement."

Numerous studies have demonstrated that exercise improves not only physical health but also mental health. This is true across cultural contexts. A 2019 analysis out of King's College London examined more than forty studies that collectively followed 267,000 people to explore the connection between exercise and depression. The researchers found that regular physical activity reduced the chances that someone would experience depression by between 17 and 41 percent, a substantial effect that was observed regardless of age and gender, and that held true across various types of movement, from running to lifting weights. Other research has found similar effects for anxiety.

Movement doesn't just help prevent mental illness; it can also treat it. In addition to their large study on prevention, the King's College researchers conducted a review of twenty-five studies that surveyed a total of 1,487 people who were currently experiencing depression. They found that between 40 and 50 percent of people with depression respond positively to exercise, with an effect that, on a scale of small, medium, or large, is considered large. Researchers from the University of Limerick in Ireland conducted their own analysis that included 922 participants and found a similar response rate for anxiety. These rates are on par with psychotherapy and medication.*

---

*It is important to note that exercise is not a panacea for mental health issues. While exercise can and often does help, this is not always the case for everyone. I know many people who experience (or have experienced) mental illness and who rightfully get fed up when they are told, "Just exercise more." If it were that easy, everyone would do it. It is also important to note that other mental illness treatments and exercise are not mutually exclusive but can be used together to great benefit. Many of the most successful treatment regimens for mental illness involve a combination of exercise, therapy, and medication.

Movement may seem distinct from the other principles discussed in this book so far. Sadly, heroic individualism's infatuation with gut-wrenching workouts, external appearance, and "exercise" as punishment has clouded how we think about our bodies and how we ought to use them. But, as you'll soon see, genuine movement is integral to the practice of groundedness.

AN INTEGRATED MIND-BODY SYSTEM

In the 1640s, French philosopher René Descartes introduced what came to be known as Cartesian dualism, or the idea that although materially connected, the mind and body are separate entities. This thinking dominated for more than 350 years. It wasn't until the turn of the twenty-first century that scientists began to prove that Descartes was mistaken. We do not have a distinct mind and body. Rather, <u>we are an integrated mind–body system</u>.

The bacteria in our guts and the proteins secreted by our muscles affect our moods. The neurochemicals in our brains affect how much pain we feel in our backs and how fast our hearts beat. When we move our bodies regularly we do a better job of controlling our emotions, we think more creatively, and we retain more information. Though the science that integrates mind and body is relatively new, the spirit behind it is not. Long before Descartes separated the two, the ancient Greeks treated mind and body more holistically. For example, the Greeks did not detach physical education from intellectual education as we do today. Rather, the two were often taught together, as part of a philosophy summarized by the Latin words *Mens sana in corpore sano*: "a healthy mind in a healthy body."

The sixth principle of groundedness is *movement*. Movement promotes generalized well-being, strength, and stability—not just in body but also in mind. The rest of this chapter will explain how and why. First, we'll briefly explore how movement supports each of the other principles—acceptance, presence, patience, vulnerability, and deep community. Then, we'll explore concrete practices that can help you develop a regular movement practice in your own life. We'll see that movement need not be complicated or heroic and that nearly everyone—regardless of age, sex, or body type—can reap its myriad benefits.

MOVEMENT AND ACCEPTANCE

When I began training for marathons, a more experienced runner offered some words of wisdom: I would need to learn how to get comfortable with being uncomfortable. This skill is every bit as helpful off the road as it is on it.

It's not just me, and it's not just running. Ask anyone whose day regularly includes pushing their bodies and they'll likely tell you the same: A difficult conversation doesn't seem so difficult anymore. A tight deadline, not so intimidating. Relationship problems, not so problematic. While it's plausible to think that exercise simply makes you too tired to care, that's not the case. Research shows that if anything, physical activity has the opposite effect, boosting brain function and energy. The more likely scenario is that pushing your body teaches you to experience pain, discomfort, and fatigue and accept it instead of immediately reacting to it or resisting it.

Evelyn Stevens, the women's record holder for most miles cycled in an hour (29.81), says that during her hardest training intervals, "instead of thinking *I want this to be over*, I try to feel and sit with the pain. Heck, I even try to embrace it." If you resist or try to suppress the discomfort that comes with pushing your body, the discomfort generally intensifies. <u>Physical activity teaches you how to accept something for what it is, see it clearly, and then decide what to do next</u>. This is magnified in a challenging workout during the moments when you must choose whether to lay off or keep pushing.

A study published in the *British Journal of Health Psychology* found that college students who went from not exercising at all to even a modest program of two to three gym visits per week reported a decrease in stress, smoking, and alcohol and caffeine consumption, and an increase in healthy eating and better spending and study habits. In addition to these real-life improvements, after two months of regular exercise, the students also performed better on laboratory tests of self-control. This led the researchers to speculate that exercise had a powerful impact on the students' "capacity for self-regulation." In laypeople's terms, pushing through the discomfort associated with exercise—saying yes when their bodies and minds were telling them to say no—taught the students to stay cool, calm, and collected in the face of difficulty. It taught them to accept what was happening and then take wise action in accordance with their values. In the gym this often meant to keep going. Out of the gym it meant being better at managing stress, drinking less, or studying more.

Another study, this one published in the *European Journal of Applied Physiology*, evaluated how exercise changes our physiological response to stress. Researchers at the Karlsruhe Institute of Technology, in Germany, divided students into two groups at the beginning of the semester and instructed half to run twice a week for twenty weeks. At the end of the twenty weeks, which coincided with a particularly stressful time for the students—exams—the researchers had them wear monitors throughout their day-to-day activities to measure their heart-rate variability, which is a common indicator of physiological stress. As you might expect, the students who were enrolled in the running program showed more favorable heart-rate variability. Their bodies literally were not as stressed during exams. Perhaps instead of fighting the pressure surrounding exams, they were more accepting of it and thus less unsettled.

What's encouraging about these studies is that the subjects weren't exercising at heroic intensities or volumes. They were simply doing something that was physically challenging for them—going from no exercise to some exercise. A recurring theme in this chapter is that one need not be an elite athlete or fitness buff to reap the wide-ranging benefits of movement. When you develop a movement practice it is likely there will be times when you are uncomfortable. These times not only make your body stronger, but they give your mind safe and controlled opportunities to practice acceptance, to practice staying grounded during distress. For some this may require lifting lots of weight or running very fast. But for others it might simply mean going from no movement to daily thirty-minute brisk walks.

MOVEMENT AND PRESENCE

A regular movement practice teaches you that the more you treat every rep or step independently, as if it were its own workout, the better. At first this takes a lot of focus, but eventually it becomes second nature. As presence increases, not only does your experience of training improve, but so does your performance. Whatever happened on the last rep doesn't matter. Whatever happens on the next rep doesn't matter. Only this rep—the one you are currently completing—matters.

A common way for people to experience flow is through physical activity. The heightened sensations in your body provide an anchor for your awareness, and the increased arousal helps channel your mind. For this to occur, however, you need to leave the digital devices behind (or at least turn them on airplane mode if you are going to use them for music). For exercisers to experience flow, they must "keep their minds into what they are doing," writes Pirkko Markula, a professor of physical activity at the University of Alberta in Canada.

When I work with coaching clients on incorporating movement into their lives, we explicitly use it as an opportunity to experience distraction-free time. Many realize a big reason why they've come to enjoy exercising is precisely because they aren't constantly being pinged by calls, emails, or texts. The more they have this kind of distraction-free experience, the more they start to prioritize and protect presence in other areas of their lives. This parallels a theory put forth by the author and habit expert Charles Duhigg: movement is a "keystone habit," or positive practice in one area of life that brings about positive changes in others.

Movement also develops presence because it demands you pay close attention to the signals your body is sending. *Do I speed up or slow down? Is this merely the pain of arduous exertion, or is this the pain of a looming injury?* Since you receive rather concrete feedback on these decisions, you can continually refine your process. Keep doing this and your ability to pay close attention—not just as it relates to your body, but to all of life—improves.

MOVEMENT AND PATIENCE

I've had the privilege of getting to know some of the top athletes in the world. What's interesting is that they all use different strategies to build fitness. Some follow a high-intensity, low-volume approach; others, the opposite. Some train using heart-rate zones, while others use perceived exertion. And yet they've all told me that the key to training success isn't so much the plan, but whether or not they stick to it. So long as the training is based on sound principles, the specific method isn't nearly as important as an athlete's patience and consistency with it. There are many roads to Rome, but you'll only get there if you don't constantly veer off the route you chose.

The key to improving physical fitness lies in adhering to a concept called progressive overload. You work a specific muscle or function in a specific manner, progressively adding intensity and duration over time. Hard days are followed by easy days. Prolonged periods of intensity are followed by prolonged periods of recovery. Repetition and consistency are key. Results don't occur overnight but after months, and even years. As mentioned in chapter 4, if you rush the process or try to do too much too soon, your chances of injury and overtraining increase. There is no escaping or denying this. Your body simply lets you know. You learn patience, in your tendons and bones.

"Today, everyone desires novelty and endless stimulation," explains my friend Vern Gambetta, a world-renowned, "old-timer" athletic development coach who has trained hundreds of elite athletes, including members of the New York Mets and Chicago Bulls, as well as numerous Olympians. "Running around and constantly switching what you are doing from one day to the next is in vogue." But if what you're after is long-term growth and development, he says, speed and switching just don't work. Physical progress requires playing the long game.

A regular movement practice teaches you that breakthroughs do not happen overnight. They result from consistent effort applied over a long duration, from gradually pounding the stone in a smart and controlled manner until one day it breaks. Improvement in fitness requires being patient and present in the process, stopping one rep short today so that you can pick up where you left off tomorrow.

MOVEMENT AND VULNERABILITY

If you choose to challenge yourself in any kind of physical practice, there will be occasions when you fail. It's the nature of the beast. Trying to run or walk faster, lift more weight, or cycle farther than you ever have before can be at least mildly intimidating.

You are facing all sorts of unknowns. *How much discomfort will this cause? Will I be able to push through? Will I quit too early? Will I succeed or fail?*

Whenever I attempt a big lift in the gym, my training partner Justin, sensing my hesitancy, often utters the words "brave new world." Regardless of the outcome, I am practicing the art of facing vulnerabilities with courage, of learning to trust myself in challenging situations. And when I fail, sometimes in front of other people, I learn to be okay with that, too. A regular movement practice exposes where you are weak and teaches you not to run away from those areas but to turn toward and work on them instead. The more you confront your weaknesses the stronger and more integrated you become, in the most literal sense.

In the weight room (or on the track, playing field, or in the pool) it is just you and the bar. You either make the lift or you don't. If you make it, great. If not, you train more and try again. Some days it goes well; other days it doesn't. But over time, it becomes clear that what you get out of yourself is proportional to the effort you put in, and to your willingness to expose yourself to ever-increasing trials and sometimes come up short. It's as simple and as hard as that. You develop a kind of vulnerability, straightforwardness, and self-reliance in the midst of challenge that gives rise to a quiet and secure confidence. You learn to trust yourself and take risks in the presence of others, which is precisely how you forge more intimate bonds in your movement community.

MOVEMENT AND DEEP COMMUNITY

A growing body of research shows that exercising with other people promotes connection and belonging, or what we've been calling deep community. In her book *The Joy of Movement*, health psychologist and Stanford lecturer Kelly McGonigal details the many reasons this is the case. There is the collective joy our species is hardwired to feel when we move in synchrony with others, a phenomenon that at first was an evolutionary advantage that promoted cooperation during hunting. There is the release of neurochemicals such as endorphins and oxytocin, which promote affection and bonding. There is the ritualistic nature intrinsic to many exercise programs, leading to a sensation scientists call *identity fusion*—feeling connected to and part of something larger than oneself. And there is the shared confidence, vulnerability, and trust that emerges from undertaking physical challenges with others. Exercise scientists refer to this as "muscular bonding," likely for its long-standing application as a rite of passage in tribal cultures and, more recently, in the military.

"We crave this feeling of connection," says McGonigal, "and synchronized movement is one of the most powerful ways to experience it." She writes that outsiders often fail to understand the social effects of movement. "Like any nature-harnessing phenomenon, it doesn't make sense until you're in the middle of it. Then suddenly, endorphins flowing and heart pounding, you find [the kind of belonging that exercise gives rise to] the most reasonable thing in the world."

I've come to know this firsthand. Rarely have I regretted the additional effort it takes to coordinate schedules in order to run, hike, or lift weights with others. The short-term effect is that I always feel better afterward. The long-term effect is that some of my best friends are people whom I first met in the gym or on the trail.

Now that we've established the benefits of movement, we'll turn to its application. Unfortunately, when it comes to movement there is a deluge of misinformation out there, or what I've come to call "bro-science": complex-sounding jargon—usually, but not always, peddled by people looking to make a buck—that lacks substance and effectiveness. It's heroic individualism in a fitness flavor. I can't stand that stuff. Rest assured, what I offer will be different. I'll review simple and concrete movement practices that actually work. All are backed by years of evidence and real-world experience. All can be customized to fit into your own life. And all are free. But before we get into those concrete practices, I want to explain one of the most important and beneficial mindset shifts you can make when it comes to your health, well-being, and pursuit of genuine success. For many, adopting this mindset serves as the bedrock of any enduring movement practice.

MAKE MOVEMENT A PART OF YOUR JOB—WHATEVER YOUR JOB (AND FITNESS LEVEL) MAY BE

But I don't have time. It's the most common excuse I hear for not engaging in regular physical activity. While this may be true if you are working multiple jobs and struggling to meet your basic needs, it is simply not true for the majority of people. A 2019 study by the Centers for Disease Control and Prevention (CDC) in partnership with the think tank RAND asked a diverse sample of 32,000 Americans about the use of their time. They found that, on average, Americans have more than 4.5 hours per day of leisure time, the vast majority of which is spent sitting in front of screens. This finding was consistent across income, age, gender, and ethnicity. Even if you insist that you are too busy to move your body because you work an important and intense job, I would strongly consider reframing physical activity not as something you do separate from your job, but rather as an integral part of your job. This is true if you are a physician, nurse, lawyer, investor, teacher, writer, researcher, parent—pretty much anyone.

Research shows that regular physical activity increases creative thinking and problem solving, improves mood and emotional control, enhances focus and energy, and promotes quality sleep. There is no line of work that doesn't benefit from these attributes. Three neurotransmitters—serotonin, norepinephrine, and dopamine—are integral to brain function. Serotonin influences mood, norepinephrine heightens perception, and dopamine regulates attention and satisfaction. When these neurotransmitters are in balance, the brain is ready for optimal functioning. When they are out of balance, cognitive and emotional capacity suffer, and in severe cases, psychiatric disorders may arise. Physical activity is special because it seems to promote an ideal balance of these three neurotransmitters. When you move your body, you move your mind, too.

Consider a study from Stanford University. Aptly titled "Give Your Ideas Some Legs," it asked participants to engage in mentally fatiguing tasks. One group took a break during which the participants sat and stared at a wall. Another group went on a six-to fifteen-minute walk during their break. After the break, both groups were tested for their creative insight. The participants who took the short walk demonstrated a 40 percent increase in creative insight over those who didn't. This effect isn't confined to adults. Other studies have found that when youth engage in regular physical activity, their academic performance improves. The great irony is that so many schools cut physical activity in favor of math, science, and standardized test prep, when physical activity may be the very thing that would help students improve their math, science, and scores on standardized tests, not to mention help with economically devastating health care costs and public health problems.

In addition to facilitating your brain's performance today, physical activity simultaneously helps your brain perform better tomorrow. Movement promotes long-term brain development by triggering the release of a chemical called brain-derived neurotrophic factor (BDNF). BDNF is like fertilizer for the brain. It fuels a process called neurogenesis, which spawns new brain cells and makes connections between them. The link between physical activity and BDNF helps explain mounting evidence that regular movement prevents and delays cognitive decline. The effect is so powerful that, to date, there is no better prevention for neurodegenerative diseases like Alzheimer's and Parkinson's than regular physical activity. If movement could be bottled and sold in pill form it would be a trillion-dollar blockbuster drug—used for everything from enhancing performance to improving well-being to preventing and treating disease.

It is for all these reasons that I prioritize physical activity in my coaching practice. Once my clients begin to view physical activity as an essential part of their jobs, they are more likely to make it a regular part of their lives. This shift in mindset provides many of my clients with both the permission and motivation to spend time moving their bodies. They go from seeing movement as something that is self-serving or not mission critical to seeing it as indispensable.

This mindset shift is occurring at even the most elite levels of cognitive competition. In 2019, ESPN.com published a story exploring how world-class chess masters often lose ten to fifteen pounds during a weeklong tournament. According to scientists, this is related to the human stress response. During tournaments, which can last five to ten days, it is not uncommon for competitors to experience elevated heart rates, high blood pressure, obsessive thinking, emotional and physiological anxiety, loss of appetite, crippling doubt, and insomnia. As a result, world-class chess players are beginning to train their bodies as if they were world-class athletes. They are adopting intense fitness regimens so that they can think more clearly and maintain strength and stability during the ongoing distress of a tournament. "Physical fitness and brain performance are tied together, and it shouldn't be a surprise that grandmasters are out there trying to look like soccer players," says chess superstar Maurice Ashley.

Shifting your mindset to view exercise as a part of your job is a good start, but you still need to execute on it. There are two main ways to integrate movement into your life:

- You can set aside a protected time for physical activity such as walking, running, cycling, swimming, gardening, climbing, dancing, going to the gym, or yoga.

- You can build movement into the regular flow of your day.

At a minimum, you want to be consistent about at least one of these ways. Ideally, you'll use a combination of both. For example, perhaps you go to the gym or work out in your basement three days per week, go for a longer walk or hike on the weekend, and then try to stay generally active on all the other days. But there is no magic formula. When it comes to movement, my golden rule is this: *Move your body often*, *sometimes hard*; *every bit counts.*

The following practices will help you to integrate movement into your day and also learn how to get the most out of formal periods of exercise. We'll bust common myths such as that you need to be athletic to exercise; strength training is only for young people; higher intensity is always better; and good workouts require a lot of equipment and time. We'll also detail the evidence-based information that can help you create your own customized movement practice.

PRACTICE: MOVE THROUGHOUT THE DAY

That we even need to "exercise" is a recent phenomenon. Before the Industrial Revolution, we worked on farms. And before that we were hunters and gatherers. Our species has had the opportunity to be sedentary for only 0.1 percent of its existence. Put differently, if you think of the human species up to this point as existing over a twenty-four-hour day, it wasn't until 11:58 p.m. that we stopped moving regularly. We were born to move, and that's certainly how we have evolved.

It is not surprising, then, that going without movement for extended periods of time is harmful. A meta-analysis that reviewed thirteen studies found that those who sat for more than eight hours per day with no physical activity had a risk of dying similar to the risks posed by obesity and smoking. Sitting for more than eight hours per day is associated with increased blood pressure, increased blood sugar, excess body fat, depression, heart disease, and cancer. While these maladies make you more likely to sit, there is also evidence that sitting makes you more likely to develop these maladies. In other words, sitting isn't just a symptom of so many health problems, but also an underlying cause. Other studies show that even if you exercise during protected times (e.g., your thirty-minute run or yoga class), sitting for long periods is still detrimental to your physical health.

As mentioned earlier, extensive sitting also hurts mental performance. Regular movement increases blood flow to the brain. It also gives the thinking parts of your brain a chance to rest while the parts that coordinate movement come online. In combination, these two mechanisms explain why movement is so beneficial for cognition and creativity.

Fortunately, it does not take much to counter the negative effects of sitting. A study published in the *Journal of the American Heart Association* found that walking for just two minutes every hour countered most of the harmful effects of sitting. The same goes for taking three ten-minute walks per day. The sweet spot, however, may actually be somewhere in between.

For a 2016 study published in the *International Journal of Behav-*

ioral Nutrition and Physical Activity, researchers from the University of Colorado and the Johnson & Johnson Human Performance Institute set out to test the effects of a variety of movement protocols on office workers. The participants came to a lab in which they simulated a six-hour workday under three conditions: During one visit, participants sat for the entire six hours other than to take bathroom breaks. During another visit, the participants went on a thirty-minute walk to begin the day and then sat for five and a half hours consecutively (again, getting up only for bathroom breaks). In the third visit, participants walked for five minutes every hour, in essence repeating cycles of sitting and working for fifty-five minutes and then walking for five.

The results showed that participants fared better on nearly all measures of well-being and performance when they had some kind of movement baked into their day, whether it was a single thirty-minute walk or six five-minute walks. Across the board, their self-reported mood and energy levels were higher, and their biological markers of health were better. There were some differences between the two movement conditions, though. During the simulated workday that included repeated five-minute walks, the participants reported greater overall satisfaction and more energy. They also reported feeling more consistently upbeat throughout the day, whereas on the day participants took a single thirty-minute walk, their energy peaked earlier. The researchers concluded that while all movement is good movement, breaking up your day with five-minute bouts of physical activity every hour or so may be best for overall performance and well-being. Creatives, intellectuals, and those who work in a traditional workplace should consider working in intervals: focus hard for a period of time; take a short break during which you engage in some sort of physical activity; rinse and repeat. This is not only how you get the most out of your body but also how you get the most out of your mind.

The aforementioned studies focused on walking, but there seems to be no reason that the same benefits wouldn't be true for other forms of movement, such as push-ups, squats, or yoga. Whether done in two-minute, five-minute, or ten-minute bursts, the message is clear: small micro-movements throughout the day add up. Per the golden rule of physical activity, *move your body often, sometimes hard; every bit counts.* Here are a few ways that you can work movement into the flow of your day:

- Put on and take off your shoes while standing up.

- Use the stairs instead of elevators or escalators.

- If possible, consider an active commute (e.g., walking or biking to work).

- If you drive to work, intentionally park far away from the building entrance.

- Always keep a water bottle nearby. You'll drink more, which means you'll need to pee more, which means you'll get up and move more in order to get to the bathroom.

- Instead of booking meetings for thirty or sixty minutes, book them for twenty-five or fifty minutes. Use the time you save for short movement breaks.

- Schedule walking meetings. Remember, research shows walking increases creativity and problem solving. If you're worried you might forget key points, simply bring a small notebook with you.

- When you feel yourself getting stuck on a problem or thought, instead of continuing to lean into it, use that feeling of being stuck as a cue to lean out and take a short break, during which you move. Not only does the research support this, but my guess is that your personal experience does, too. Think about when you tend to have moments of insight. Do they happen when you're actively working on the problem you are trying to solve? Or do they happen during a break, when you are doing something else?

- If you struggle with these suggestions and are someone who responds well to rigid rules, set an alarm to go off on the hour, notifying you to take a movement break. The key, of course, is that you can't constantly ignore these notifications or put them off.

The point isn't to do anything heroic or radical. Rather, it is to seamlessly work movement into your day, remembering it fosters strength, stability, and health not just for your body but also for your mind.

PRACTICE: GET AEROBIC

When I lived in Oakland, California, I spent a lot of time at Lake Merritt, which was about a quarter of a mile down Grand Avenue from my apartment. An adjacent footpath circumnavigates the lake and is exactly 3.1 miles long. If I was out there on a Tuesday, Thursday, or Saturday morning, I would inevitably bump into Ken. It was impossible not to. Ken, an older gentleman with thin white hair down to his shoulders, always wore gray cotton shorts, a faded sweatshirt, and New Balance shoes that were falling apart. He walked three laps around the lake—or 9.3 miles—on each of those days. One day, I stopped my run to ask Ken his age. "Ninety-something," he replied. When I asked him his secret, how he's still doing what he's doing, he told me it's what he's always been doing. "I've been walking out here for years and years," he said. "You've just got to keep moving." Ken was imparting some serious fitness wisdom.

Aerobic fitness refers to your body's ability to use oxygen efficiently. Higher levels of aerobic fitness are associated with just about every positive physical and mental health outcome imaginable. Though it's easy to get excited about the latest and greatest trends, from high-intensity interval training to ultramarathons to triathlons, at the end of the day, regular brisk walking gets you most, if not all, of the way there—"there" meaning fit for a long, healthy, and satisfying life. This was the conclusion in a special edition of the *British Journal of Sports Medicine* (*BJSM*) in 2019 that was dedicated to walking.

"Whether it is a stroll on a sunny day, walking to and from

work, or walking down to the local shops, the act of putting one foot in front of the other in a rhythmic manner is as much human nature as breathing, thinking and loving," write Emmanuel Stamatakis, Mark Hamer, and Marie Murphy in an editorial accompanying their original research.

The main study in the *BJSM* special edition surveyed more than fifty thousand walkers in the United Kingdom across a variety of ages. It found that regularly walking at an average, brisk, or fast pace was associated with a 20 percent reduction in all-cause mortality and a 24 percent reduction in the risk of dying from cardiovascular disease. "A very simple way to grasp a 'brisk' pace in terms of exertion is to imagine it as a pace that gets you out of breath when it is sustained for more than a few minutes," says Stamatakis, lead author on the study and professor of physical activity, lifestyle, and population health at the University of Sydney, in Australia.

Another 2019 study, published in the *American Journal of Preventive Medicine*, examined nearly 140,000 men and women in the United States and came to the same conclusion. Engaging in at least 150 minutes per week of brisk walking was linked to a 20 percent reduction in all-cause mortality. A common challenge to these big, population-wide studies is that they don't measure causation. While regular walking promotes good health, it could also be that you can't walk regularly or briskly if you're not in good health. However, both of these studies went to great lengths to control for participants' baseline health. Meanwhile, many smaller studies designed as randomized controlled trials—meaning some subjects are assigned to walk and others aren't—show that walking causes improvements in health. When you combine all of this research, you can become pretty confident that walking leads to good health, not the other way around.

Walking has also been compared to more intense forms of exercise, like running. Though experts believe running may be marginally better for you, that's only if you don't get injured and if you manage to run regularly, something with which more than 50 percent of runners (me included) have struggled. If you enjoy and are able to stick to more strenuous forms of aerobic physical activity, by all means, do those. Regular running, cycling, swimming, and dancing are all extremely beneficial. But do not fret if you find yourself frequently injured or lacking the time, equipment, access, or motivation to participate in higher-intensity activities. Most people can walk briskly for thirty to forty-five minutes a day and achieve loads of health benefits. If you do it regularly over the course of your lifetime, there's compelling evidence that it might be the only aerobic exercise you need.

While the science surrounding aerobic fitness is relatively new, its conclusions are not. In the early 1800s, in a letter to his sister, who was struggling with both her physical and mental health, Danish philosopher Søren Kierkegaard wrote, "Above all, do not lose your desire to walk: every day I walk myself into a state of well-being and walk away from every illness; I have walked myself into my best thoughts, and I know of no thought so burdensome that one cannot walk away from it."

Whether you choose to walk or participate in another form of aerobic movement, a few ground rules can help. Many of these also apply to strength training, which is the movement practice we'll turn to next.

- Schedule formal workouts on your calendar.* If you don't prioritize and protect time for them, they won't happen. Treat workouts like important meetings with yourself—because that's precisely what they are. Outside of family emergencies nothing encroaches on my workout time. I don't think that is because I am crazy but rather because my workouts help keep me sane.

- The best time to work out is the time that you'll consistently stick with. Some people prefer working out in the morning, others during lunch, and still others in the evening. There is no compelling evidence that says any of these times are better than the others.

- Start small and gradually build in frequency, duration, and intensity. This will help protect against both physical and emotional injury from doing too much too soon. A reasonable starting point for most people is to aim for two to three formal aerobic workouts a week, ranging from thirty to sixty minutes each—long enough to get a big benefit, short enough to fit into your day.

- If you live somewhere with harsh winters and want to walk or run year-round, consider using a treadmill. If that's not possible or appealing, you can go to your local mall and use it as an indoor track. Many indoor malls, especially in cold areas, open early for walkers. Some even organize walking groups.

---

*I include brisk walking in my definition of a workout.

- Whenever possible, try to work out with other people for all of the reasons mentioned earlier, in the community subsection of this chapter.

There is one more important point when it comes to aerobic activity. While all movement is good movement, if you can, try to do at least some of it outdoors. There is mounting evidence that being in nature augments both the physical and psychological benefits of exercise. When you consider the deep history of our species, this makes sense. As with being sedentary, urban and suburban indoor living is a relatively new phenomenon for humans. The biophilia hypothesis, made popular by the Harvard entomologist E. O. Wilson, states that we evolved to have an innate tendency to seek connections with nature and other forms of life. Wilson believes that since our species evolved outside in nature, we are biologically programmed to be drawn to it. In other words, a longing for nature may literally be in our DNA—we're hardwired to feel at home and at ease not in the city or in the suburbs, but in nature.

Research from Japan supports Wilson's hypothesis. There, scientists have taken hundreds of individuals on "forest walks," or leisurely strolls through lush green spaces. Before and after these walks, the researchers measured a variety of bioindicators in the participants related to stress. They've found that, compared to urban walks, forest walks have a significantly more positive effect: they reduce stress levels, diminish sympathetic nerve activity, and decrease both blood pressure and heart rate. Other research, out of Stanford University, found that after a ninety-minute nature walk versus an urban walk of the same duration, people not only self-reported decreased rumination, but they also demonstrated decreased neural activity in the part of the brain associated with anxiety and depression. Thanks to urban-walk control groups, the researchers were able to account for the positive effects of aerobic exercise and isolate the unique and additional benefits of nature.

All of this makes me think ninety-something-year-old Ken really did have it figured out. He walked regularly; he walked at a pace that felt challenging for him; he walked in his community; and he walked outside around a lake. Though he might not have known it, Ken followed one of the best aerobic fitness regimens there is.

PRACTICE: STRENGTH TRAINING

Contrary to what you may think, strength training is not just for the tank-topped muscle heads at your local gym. It's for everyone. Some of the largest research consortiums, such as the American Heart Association, recommend strength training at least twice a week regardless of age or gender. As with aerobic movement, in addition to supporting increased muscle mass, lower body fat, and better range of motion, research shows strength training also promotes sound mental health and cognitive performance.

While strength training can be undertaken at a gym and involve all kinds of equipment, for many people that environment is intimidating, at least at first. It is also true that gyms have membership fees and require additional commuting time. By no means am I making the case against training at a gym. I love my local gym, the community I've built there, and the additional accountability it brings. The membership fee is probably the single best use of my money. If you are interested in joining a gym I'd highly recommend following that interest. I'm simply stating that you don't need to have a gym membership to strength-train, something many people have been forced to realize during the COVID-19 pandemic, which temporarily closed gyms around the world. There are plenty of strength movements that can be performed with a twenty-five-dollar kettlebell or nothing but your own body weight.

Taken together, these movements work all the major muscle groups, use your full range of motion, and can easily be adapted to different environments and fitness and skill levels. During the COVID-19 pandemic I (and many of my coaching clients) did variations of these movements for multiple months in my home or outdoors in uncrowded spaces. You can do a few sets of each individually or combine them in a circuit. If you have a kettlebell or weights, you can add those if you wish to increase the challenge.*

- Squats

- Push-ups

- Step-ups

- Lunges

- Glute raises

- Wall sits

- Planks

- Sit-ups

- Dips

- Curls (if you don't have a weight you can use a full backpack)

- Burpees

* This is not meant to be medical advice. Always check with your doctor before starting a new workout routine. For more on simple but effective strength workouts, see "The Minimalist's Strength Workout," a popular story I wrote for *Outside* magazine published in October 2017.

FINAL THOUGHTS ON MOVEMENT

Movement has been an essential part of our species' history. Only recently have sedentary lifestyles in the name of so-called efficiency taken hold, the rise of which parallels the rise of chronic disease, mental illness, and burnout. By no means is movement a panacea for all that ails us, but it can certainly help. In addition to supporting physical health, mental health, and well-being, movement reinforces all the other principles of groundedness. It teaches us to accept discomfort, to be present in our bodies, to be patient and consistent on the slow path to progress, and to be vulnerable when we are challenging ourselves and risking failure. It is also a powerful way to build deep community and forge connections. When you regularly move your body, you come to more fully inhabit it, wherever you are. For all of these reasons, to be grounded is to move.

Part Two

LIVING A GROUNDED LIFE

8

FROM PRINCIPLES
TO ACTION

I t is one thing to understand the principles of groundedness; it is another to make them real and to align your daily habits and activities with them. You don't become what you think. You become what you do. Living a grounded life starts with a mindset shift, but it continues as an ongoing practice. If you want to get strong you can't just read about and study weight lifting. You actually have to lift the weights. That's just the way it goes, and the same applies here.

It is also true that in order to transition to a more grounded life, you may face resistance, both personal and cultural, especially since today's society—and the heroic individualism it espouses—is in opposition to cultivating and nourishing the principles of groundedness. We've become so consumed with superficial and external endpoints like greatness, immortality, and bliss—trying to hack our way to happiness, preoccupied with marginal gains, and obsessed with optimization—that we've forgotten to pay attention to the foundational principles that keep us healthy, solid, fulfilled, and strong.

Anytime you attempt a significant change there will be resistance, usually commensurate with the size of the change; it's part of the process. The rest of this chapter will help you understand how to harmoniously integrate all the principles of groundedness into your life, including common pitfalls and how to overcome them.

As you read on, remember that some days will be good. Some days will be bad. Most days will be somewhere in between. The goal is not to be the best or perfect. The goal is to give an honest effort, to incrementally become more grounded. Let's start now.

MASTER THE BEING-DOING CYCLE

I've long been working on the principles of groundedness with a coaching client named Parker, a chief information officer (CIO) at a large professional services firm. We started working together shortly after Parker was promoted into his leadership role. He was excited about the job, albeit a little overwhelmed. Though he had managed large teams before, he had never been in a position where his responsibility wasn't just to lead individual people, but also to lead an entire technology organization, including setting a comprehensive innovation and data science strategy. This required balancing daily tasks with an ability to step back, see and think clearly, and influence people en masse. Parker had to not only be in the dance but also orchestrate it, a hard-earned skill that, in reality, benefits everyone, whether you are leading an entire organization or simply leading yourself.

I quickly found Parker to be one of my most thoughtful and intellectual clients. He is a rigorous thinker who loves to read and watch documentaries in his spare time. Parker's goals focused on becoming a calm and collected leader. He wanted to achieve influence via respect, not fear or authority. He also sought to maintain his health and family life, even as a new CIO. He yearned to push forward but without losing ground, and he was excited to release from the pressures of heroic individualism.

It wasn't long before Parker fully internalized all the principles of groundedness. He dedicated time for the formal practices and found the mindfulness, wise observer, and facing your insecurities exercises especially helpful. As a result, he not only understood the principles intellectually, but he began to feel a big difference, too. There was only one problem: when Parker wasn't actively reflecting on the principles of groundedness at home or in session with me, he'd all too easily get caught up in the tumult of his day-to-day work and start feeling off again, only to reset and feel better after our next coaching session. This cycle repeated for a few months, until in one coaching session he said something along the lines of, "I feel like I know this stuff deep down inside. I just need to do it more consistently and in more situations. I just need to do it." I smiled at him and he smiled back. We both knew the path forward.

Though Parker's insight was spot-on, executing wouldn't be easy. He was coming face-to-face with the same resistance that I face, that you'll face, and that anyone reading this book will confront.

Your inner way of being influences what you do, but what you do also influences your inner way of being. Parker was falling into a common trap. He was spending a lot of time and energy on the internal work and formal practices, on strengthening his internal groundedness, but he wasn't necessarily manifesting these qualities in his everyday actions. His being was out of alignment with his doing. Instead of a harmonious feedback loop—in which being strengthens doing and doing strengthens being—Parker was stuck in gridlock. Too many of his daily activities and routines ran counter to the principles of a more grounded life.

Earlier on we discussed cognitive dissonance, or the tension and distress that emerges when you have inconsistencies between your thoughts, feelings, and beliefs on the one hand and your actions on the other. The discomfort that accompanies cognitive dissonance serves as an alert that you either need to change your thoughts, feelings, and beliefs to better reflect your actions, or you need to change your actions to better reflect your thoughts, feelings, and beliefs. Put more simply, experiencing cognitive dissonance is often a sign that you need to better align your *being* and your *doing*. In Parker's case, he was confident in his being, but he needed to bring more intentionality to his daily actions.

When you align your doing with your being, the tension of cognitive dissonance dissipates. Instead of fighting against yourself, you'll find your actions start to flow more freely. You'll begin to feel more integrated and whole. In a famous sermon to his disciples in the early 1300s, the spiritual teacher and mystic Meister Eckhart implored of his followers: "It is not that we should abandon, neglect, or deny our inner self, but we should learn to work precisely in it, with it, and from it in such a way that *interiority turns into effective action and effective action leads back to interiority* and **we become used to acting without any compulsion**" (emphasis added).

For nearly everyone I know, myself included, the last part of Eckhart's doctrine can be the hardest. How do we shift the inertia, or what Eckhart called the compulsive action, of our long-standing and habitual ways of doing? Following through on this shift is probably the least inspirational and invigorating part of making big changes. It is also perhaps the most important.

WEAVING THE PRINCIPLES OF GROUNDEDNESS TOGETHER

In my work with Parker we identified areas in which his habitual doing was most out of alignment with his emerging way of being. For example, he was regularly working at night, though he knew he wasn't at his best then; not to mention working at that hour caused him stress, made him feel scattered, and interrupted his sleep. He was avoiding difficult conversations with colleagues, especially those who had been peers before his promotion to CIO. He was focusing on too many initiatives at once and this made him feel chronically rushed, like he was always falling behind. He was suffering from impostor syndrome, trying to act more confident than he really was, even though he deeply wanted to put all of that aside and be himself. He wasn't exercising consistently even though he knew how much better he felt—and performed—when he regularly moved his body. And last but not least, he felt relatively isolated from CIOs at other organizations—like there was more he could be doing to learn from leaders who had been in his shoes before.

Parker and I decided to shift the focus of our coaching sessions. We would spend less time on understanding and strategy and more time on blocking and tackling; we would focus on where the rubber meets the road. For each of the areas Parker was struggling with, we worked out what kind of doing would be more in alignment with his new way of being. Here's a rough list of what we came up with:

- Turn his phone off during dinner. (presence)

- Take up woodworking again, one of his past loves and a gateway to flow from before he was promoted to CIO. Practically, this meant getting to his basement shop at least three nights a week. (presence)

- Walk for an hour at least three days per week. (movement)

- Make a list of the difficult conversations he needed to have, accept these would be challenging and awkward, and have them anyway. Stop kicking the can down the road. (acceptance)

- Never bring his phone into his bedroom at night. When that wasn't enough, we shifted to leaving it downstairs. This way he wouldn't check it when he got up to go to the bathroom, something he had been doing automatically and that resulted in his mind racing and trouble falling back asleep. (presence)

- Own his experience in presentations to his firm's board of directors, but don't be scared to openly admit his uncertainties where he had them. Stop shying away from the phrases "It depends" and "I don't know, let's discuss." (vulnerability)

- Focus on no more than three priorities each week. For each priority, come up with a few key actions. Write both the priorities and actions on a notecard and stick it to his desk. Resist the temptation to engage in whatever novel opportunities arise—because they are always arising—and focus on the long game instead. (patience)

- Attend more conferences and CIO gatherings where he could learn from veteran leaders and feel supported. (deep community)

Parker's struggle is not uncommon. Another one of my coaching clients, Samantha, is the founder and CEO of a company dedicated to helping workplace professionals perform their best and feel their best. Like Parker, Samantha quickly understood all the principles in this book. We even worked together to bake them into her company's curriculum. However, that did not change the fact that Samantha, a former Division 1 athlete in her thirties with a history of perfectionism, was growing a company with venture capital funding—and was also the mother of a nine-month-old. In short, she had a lot going on. Meaningful change was going to be challenging. Though the company she built is dedicated to helping people perform from a place of wholeness and freedom, Samantha herself sometimes felt fragile and tight.

Just the fact that Samantha admitted this to me, through teary eyes, was a huge step. She was trying to be a strong and bulletproof leader of a growing company, a strong and bulletproof partner to her husband, and a strong and bulletproof mother all at the same time. She felt as if she was chronically under a heavy load: all the people who were depending on her. I shared with Samantha that I, too, often feel that kind of load. Not in the same way, of course. But there are plenty of times when I feel like I need to be the person who has it together, who has all the answers for everyone else, especially when it comes to important issues. It may look like it's fun to be that person—and sometimes it is—but it can also be very exhausting.

We discussed how it can be the internal holding of that load that is heavy, not the load itself. That's when things clicked for Samantha. She was paying lip service to vulnerability but she wasn't expressing it—not to herself and certainly not to those around her. As a result, she tended to move at too fast a pace (perhaps to mask her fears and insecurities), and she sometimes got stuck performing from a place of fear more so than from a place of love. She recognized that her expectations were so absurdly high that she would never feel satisfied; she would never feel like she was enough. Ironically, it was these high expectations and subsequent feelings of never being enough that were holding Samantha back. We committed to integrating the principles of groundedness into her life by doing the following:

- Remind herself daily that founding and leading a start-up is hard. The vast majority of companies fail. That's start-up math. The fact that her company has made it this far and is still going strong is already a significant feat. This is especially true given Samantha's company had built the capital and culture to withstand the COVID-19 market downturn. On her bathroom mirror she wrote: "Stop trying not to lose. Play to win." It served as a helpful reminder every morning. (acceptance)

- Meditate for ten minutes every day. Create the time and space to get in touch with the awareness that is underneath the thinking, questioning, and doubting brain. Remember that clear-seeing awareness helps separate signal from noise. The more you practice using it, the stronger and more accessible it becomes. (presence)

- Cease paying so much attention to what other start-ups around her are doing. The result of this is that she just bounces from idea to idea. Stay focused on her mission and goals. Don't ignore the market, but don't feel the need to react to it either. Every time she feels tempted to make a reactionary move, go back to her mission and goals and ask: *Does this really help move the needle?* (patience)

- When she is struggling and feeling insecure, name what is happening and communicate it, first to herself, and then to her support system. In Samantha's case this meant me, her husband, and a few close friends and colleagues. Remember that it is okay to not be okay. Problems arise when you are not okay with not being okay, and when you don't seek support. (vulnerability and deep community)

- Shift from needing to be an all-star athlete to exercising for its mind-body benefits. Stop measuring workouts. Don't worry about training for any specific goal. Don't let physical activity be another thing she feels the need to be great at all the time. Realize the self-imposed pressure in this domain of her life is not serving her and let go of it. As a good friend of mine once said, stop trying to win at your hobby. (movement)

None of the changes that Parker or Samantha made amount to rocket science. But implementing them made a world of difference. After a few months of working toward these changes, Parker was less restless, more energized, and increasingly unfazed by events that historically would have thrown him off balance. He was sleeping better too. Even his doctor was pleased: just one year after being promoted to a stressful job, Parker's blood pressure was the lowest it had been in more than a decade. Samantha started to feel a renewed sense of lightness, like she was releasing pressure from her overfilled pot. She realized that not always having it together isn't something to fear or avoid. Rather, it is the human condition. Samantha still has periods during which she is insecure and tight, but instead of resisting these feelings she accepts them. As a result, they tend to be less intense and of a shorter duration. More of her time and energy is spent playing to win.

Choose Simplicity over Complexity

Simple changes like the ones that Parker and Samantha made can be extremely powerful—precisely because they are so simple. We often make things more complex than they need to be as a way to avoid the reality that what really matters for behavior change is consistently showing up and doing the work. Not dreaming about it. Not thinking about it. Not talking about it. Doing it.

The more complex you make something, the easier it is to get excited about, talk about, and maybe even get started—but the harder it is to stick with over the long haul. Complexity gives you excuses and ways out and endless options for switching things up all the time. Simplicity is different. You can't hide behind simplicity. You have to show up, day in and day out, and work toward your desired changes. Your successes hit you in the face. But so do your failures. This kind of quick and direct feedback allows you to learn what works and adjust what doesn't.

WORKING WITH HABIT ENERGY

You've probably heard that it takes twenty-one days to create a new habit. This myth was born in the 1950s when a plastic surgeon named Maxwell Maltz noticed that his patients acclimated to their new faces after three weeks. Maltz also found twenty-one days to be about how long it took him to groove into new routines in his own life. He wrote this down and published it in 1960, in a book called *Psycho-Cybernetics*, which went on to sell millions of copies. While Maltz's findings were fascinating, the only problem is his observations were just that, the observations of one person. Data is not the plural of anecdote.

Decades later, researchers have evaluated habit formation in a more rigorous and scientific manner. For a 2009 study published in the *European Journal of Social Psychology*, researchers from University College London tracked ninety-six people as they tried to form a new habit—what the researchers called "reaching automaticity"— related to eating, drinking, or some other specific activity. You can think about automaticity as initiating an action with little thought, effort, or internal resistance—or in our terms, when being and doing are flowing effortlessly. On average, it took participants sixty-six days to form a new habit. At an individual level, however, the range was broad. Some people took just eighteen days, while others took more than two hundred. Most of us want to be on the far left of that curve.

Developing new habits (or stopping old ones) is hard. We are creatures of routine. This is reflected by a term in ancient Eastern psychology called *habit energy*, which refers to the personal and social inertia that shapes much of our everyday doing. Habit energy is the way that we've always done things and what the culture implicitly and explicitly promotes. It is the current that drives our lives. "Habit energy is stronger than we are," says Zen master Thich Nhat Hanh. "It is pushing us all the time." Fighting against habit energy is akin to swimming against the current; it is an exhausting and losing endeavor. Fortunately, we don't always need to fight against habit energy. We can shape it to work in our favor, to support the integration of our being and doing.

The most recent psychological science supports the age-old concept of habit energy. It shows that relying on willpower alone to grind your way to new habits lowers both performance and sustainability. Constantly fighting against temptations to engage in old behaviors is draining. If you are always exerting willpower, eventually it wears out—plus, ceaselessly battling yourself doesn't make for a particularly peaceful existence. A far better approach to habit change is to minimize the need for willpower, or even better, to eliminate it altogether. Here's how this works: Reflect on the behaviors—the everyday doing—that you want (or don't want) to engage in. Then, set up the conditions conducive to those behaviors. Identify the obstacles that get in your way, the stuff that repeatedly taxes your willpower, and do what you can to remove those obstacles. Think of it like this: no matter how much you want to eat wholesome and nourishing foods, if you are constantly in a candy store you are going to eat a lot of candy. You've got to step outside the candy store.

On the flip side, also identify the people, places, and objects that support your desired behaviors and make them a more prominent part of your life. If you surround yourself wisely you become less reliant on your individual will.

Since all the principles of groundedness are interrelated, as you go through this process for more and more of your behaviors, each subsequent adjustment gets easier. In essence, you are shifting the current—your habit energy—to move in the direction of a more grounded life. Once that shift occurs you start flowing with the current instead of fighting against it. Your being and doing more easily and naturally align. You could call this living a grounded lifestyle. The following practices will help you make this shift.

PRACTICE: ALIGN YOUR *DOING* WITH YOUR *BEING*

In chapter 3 we learned about a concept in Buddhist psychology called selective watering. We all possess a diverse set of latent capacities and attitudes; these are our seeds. The seeds that we water are the ones that grow. If we want to develop unshakable groundedness, formal practice is not enough; we need to water each of the seeds, or in this case, the principles we've been discussing—acceptance, presence, patience, vulnerability, deep community, and movement—in our everyday lives. Equally important, we need to stop watering the seeds in our lives that thwart the development of these principles, aspects of heroic individualism such as denial, distraction, speed for the sake of speed, arrogance, invincibility, and rote optimization of everything.

For each principle of groundedness, come up with one to three concrete actions that you can take to water it. Also come up with one to three concrete actions that it would be wise to stop. Think of each principle as a state of your inner being. Your job is to take an inventory of your everyday actions—your doing—and try to align them with your being. Be as simple and specific as possible. For example, don't think, *Use my phone less* or *Move more*. Think more in the spirit of, *Turn off my phone every night at seven p.m. and store it in my office desk drawer until seven a.m.*, or *Walk three miles every day before lunch.*

The work of Stanford researcher BJ Fogg demonstrates that successful habits have three qualities: they have an impact, you possess the skill and ability to do them, and they are behaviors that you actually want to do. The last of these qualities is particularly important. If you find yourself thinking, I *should* do this or that, those changes will probably come with a lot more resistance. It's best to start with changes that you truly want to make, even if they aren't perfect. Remember: start small, keep it simple, and stick to specifics. Here are a few examples:

- **Acceptance:** When I catch myself desperately wanting something in my life to be different, I'll pause and ask myself what advice I'd give a friend if they were in the same situation. Then, I'll follow that advice. When I know I will be in a tricky situation for reasons outside my control, I'll step back and evaluate my expectations. If they are unrealistically high, and thus I am constantly falling short and feeling disappointed, I'll change them.

- **Presence:** Instead of checking email or scrolling on social media, I'll meditate every morning before I brush my teeth. I'll use the Insight Timer app, starting with five minutes and adding one minute each week until I reach fifteen minutes. At that point, I'll reevaluate this practice.

- **Patience:** I'll practice three-by-five breathing before breakfast, lunch, and dinner. If I am out with friends or colleagues, I can explain the practice to them, or if I don't feel comfortable, I will take those meals off.

- **Vulnerability:** When my romantic partner or a good friend asks me how I am doing, I will not always say that I am feeling good. If I am feeling sad or scared I will tell them. When I feel uncomfortable and am by myself, I'll stop running away from those feelings and instead create a safe space to explore them, even if this means reaching out to someone for help.

- **Deep community:** I'll start a group that meets monthly to discuss books like this one (more on this later). I'll stop using social media on my phone because it provides easy access to the addictive type of shallow community and relevance that gets in the way of the real thing. I won't rely on willpower but will actually remove the apps.

- **Movement:** I'll never sit for more than ninety minutes straight during the day without taking at least a five-minute walking break.

Once you develop a concrete plan for how to sync your everyday doing with your inner way of being, the next step is to implement it. For many people (including me), this is the biggest challenge. During formal periods of practice our inner being usually feels solid and strong. But far too often when we get back into the hustle and bustle of daily life, that feeling fades away. Not because it is inevitable, but because our doing doesn't always reflect our being. As my coaching client Parker said, "I feel like I know this stuff deep down inside. I just need to do it more consistently." This requires shifting your habit energy.

PRACTICE: SHIFT YOUR HABIT ENERGY

Much of human action follows a predictable cycle: trigger, behavior, reward. A simple example is exercise. The trigger could be your workout program pasted to your fridge door, the behavior is going to the gym, and the reward is that you feel great once you're finished.

For behaviors that you want to do, the goal is to make triggers evident, the behavior as easy as possible to start, and the reward immediate and satisfying. For behaviors that you want to stop, it's the opposite. Bury the trigger (remove addictive apps from your phone), make the behavior hard (log out every time you use these services on the internet so you need to remember and reenter your username and password to get back in), and sit with and deeply feel the negative consequences (the unease and hollowness that follow spending an hour on these apps when you had planned on one minute). This cycle can be applied to just about anything. Define what you want to do (or cease doing), pair it with (or remove) triggers, make the behavior easy (or hard), and then realize the rewards (or consequences).

The work of Michelle Segar, a behavioral scientist at the University of Michigan in Ann Arbor, shows that habits last longer when the rewards are internal. If you're doing a task to please someone else or to earn a treat at the end of the day, you're less likely to stick to that behavior than if you're doing it because it makes you feel good and aligns with your core values. This is welcome news, because living out the principles of groundedness is satisfying in and of itself. The more you shift your outer doing (your daily habits) to align with your inner being (the principles of groundedness you wish to embody), the better you'll feel. This may not happen automatically due to the strong inertia of habit energy, but once it starts happening for a few changes, you'll have a much easier time making subsequent ones. This is the virtuous cycle of adopting a more grounded life. Every change supports the next. It gets easier as you go.

For each of the concrete actions you came up with in the prior practice, map out triggers, behaviors, and rewards that surround it. Since the most powerful rewards are internal, think about what you expect to feel when you do (or don't do) each action and how you will make sure to pause, even if only for a moment, and feel it deeply. Also consider how you can design your surroundings—people, places, and things—to make your desired actions easier. Find friction points and do what you can to smooth or remove them. In habit speak, don't underestimate the power of everything and everyone around you to act as a trigger. In ancient wisdom speak, do what you can to shift your habit energy—the current of your life—in the direction of groundedness.

Here are some illustrations of how triggers, behaviors, and rewards work, using the same examples we addressed in the previous section.

ACCEPTANCE

Behavior to start: Practice self-distancing by pretending I am giving advice to a friend.

Triggers: Obsessing about how I didn't get the promotion I wanted or getting caught up wishing I had more time to decompress before bed.

Rewards: Stop the cycle of obsession and gain a clearer and better idea of what productive actions I can take to make the situation better.

How to design your environment: Create and wear a small bracelet that reads, "This is what is happening right now. Where you are is where you are. Start there."

PRESENCE

Behavior to start: Meditate every morning instead of scrolling social media, either right before or after brushing my teeth.

Triggers: Reaching for my phone when I wake up. Brushing my teeth.

Rewards: Being more focused on what actually matters. Becoming more aware of the distractions that regularly throw me off.

How to design your environment: Make Insight Timer (or some other meditation app) the only app on the home screen of my smartphone. Take social media off my smartphone altogether. Find a friend who also wants to try this shift in behavior so we can hold each other accountable. Adopt a mindset in which I expect this to be hard at first. This way I won't quit when it is just that.

PATIENCE

Behavior to start: Three-by-five breathing.

Triggers: Meals.

Rewards: An immediate sense of accomplishment and calm. In the longer term, an emerging awareness that just because I feel restless energy doesn't mean I need to act on it. I can pause, center myself, and create some space to respond instead of reacting.

How to design your environment: Share this practice with my family so they can be supportive. Tape a small notecard to the ledge of the kitchen table where I sit that reads, "5 breaths." If I can't do this at a meal for some reason, I'll use taking a shower as another trigger.

VULNERABILITY

Behavior to start: Be more honest about how I am feeling with important others in my life; pause and respond genuinely instead of automatically saying "fine."

Triggers: When my romantic partner, Lisa, or my good friend Justin asks me how I am doing.

Rewards: Closer connection with each of them and less energy spent faking it. More confidence to be increasingly vulnerable in other areas of my life, such as work.

How to design your environment: Share with Lisa and Justin ahead of time that I am working on being more vulnerable. This will help dampen some of the initial discomfort. It will also encourage them to be increasingly vulnerable with me, creating a virtuous cycle of realness between all parties involved.

DEEP COMMUNITY

Behavior to start: Attend (or start) a monthly book club.

Triggers: The first Wednesday evening of each month. Schedule gatherings in advance for the entire year so everyone in the club and I can plan around them.

Rewards: Closer connection with like-minded others in my town. Support and accountability in applying the principles and practices of books like these. Gaining additional perspectives on the material I read.

How to design your environment: Take social media off my phone because it often cannibalizes deep community. Create a group text instead, in which members of the club and I stay in touch between formal gatherings to keep the momentum going.

MOVEMENT

Behavior to start: Never sit for more than ninety minutes straight without a five-minute walking break.

Triggers: The feeling of needing to pee or an alarm I set on my computer or phone. Also, whenever I start to feel antsy or stuck, I'll check the time and take my break if it's been an hour.

Rewards: Less stiffness, more creativity, and enhanced focus.

How to design your environment: Buy a nice water bottle that I will take with me everywhere. Keep it full. This way, I'll have to use the bathroom more, and over time I'll become less dependent on an annoying alarm. I'll also create walking routes in the places I regularly work so I won't have to think about where to go.

PRACTICE: FORMAL REFLECTION

Regularly take stock of how your *doing* is aligning with your *being*. An easy way to go about this is to journal. At the end of each week and for each principle, take just a few minutes to reflect and rate yourself on a scale of one to five for how well your doing aligns with your being. Also make a few notes on what went right, what went wrong, and how you feel. Keep everything as straightforward and simple as possible. This practice helps you identify strengths that you can build on and areas for improvement. It provides another opportunity to reflect on how you feel as you increasingly transition to a more grounded lifestyle. It also keeps a record of your journey for you to look back upon. The weeks I find myself writing down "too much time on internet news" or "not enough transition time between activities in my day" are usually the weeks when I don't feel great. Reflecting on this helps me get back on the path heading into the next week.

Over time, as your being-doing cycle becomes increasingly integrated and the principles of groundedness take hold, you might not need to engage in this practice as frequently. Your actions will start to become second nature. That's great. Even so, I'd still recommend keeping up with journaling or some other variety of formal reflection at least once per year. The value of even a few moments for reflection is incredible—perhaps more so if you share this practice with others.

PRACTICE: MAKE GROUNDEDNESS A GROUP ENDEAVOR

As you know well by now, taking on challenges with others is usually more effective and satisfying than going it alone. A great way to live out the principles of groundedness is to make it a community project. Organize a group of people who are committed to working on the principles of groundedness and meet regularly. Personally, I've found the sweet spot for this kind of group to be anywhere between two and eight people. When you meet, discuss your goals, common challenges, successes, and failures. Share your strategies and tools. Hold each other accountable, but also provide love and support when someone falters. There are countless ways to structure this. For instance, you could meet every week, every other week, or monthly and devote each gathering to a specific principle. Or you could consider a full-day retreat where each principle gets an hour of attention. The possibilities are endless.

The power and purchase of grounded success rises exponentially when it spreads. The people and organizations in your life are an enormous part of the current behind your habit energy. Just imagine how much easier it would be to adopt the principles of groundedness if your family, community groups, and colleagues adopted them too. As we saw with the Shalane Flanagan Effect from chapter 6, working on the principles of groundedness in a group will benefit not only you but also everyone else involved.

The principles of groundedness also apply at the organizational level, and the societal level, too. Organizations and cultures that value and practice acceptance, presence, patience, vulnerability, deep community, and movement (and that promote mind-body health more broadly) are organizations and cultures that thrive. I've found that regardless of the setting—from athletic teams and college departments to creative studios, small start-ups, and large corporations—people are hungry to integrate the principles of groundedness into their organizations and societies. This is not surprising. Everyone wants to experience internal strength, deep confidence, stability, and a more fulfilling kind of success, and everyone wants to be part of an organization and society that foster those experiences.

Much like at the individual level, organizational actions are best when they are simple and specific. Here are a few examples from organizations I've worked with in the past:

- *Practice acceptance* by asking, "How might we be wrong?" for all big strategic decisions. Designate specific people to play devil's advocate in high-stakes circumstances. Solicit outside perspectives on emotionally charged topics.

- *Practice presence* by removing phones and other digital devices from key meetings. Some sporting teams do the same during workouts and training sessions.

- *Practice patience* by ensuring measurement strategies reflect an emphasis on long-term growth over short-term results. Set long-term goals and then break them down into their component parts, and focus there.

- *Practice vulnerability* by embodying openness as leaders and taking the steps outlined in chapter 5 to create psychological safety.

- *Practice deep community* by offering a book club for employees. Let members of the club vote on which books to read so everyone feels ownership.

- *Practice movement* by instituting a walking-meeting-preferred policy (for those who are able) and building on-site gyms and showers. If that seems too challenging, partner with your local gym to offer free memberships for all your employees.

FINAL THOUGHTS ON MOVING FROM PRINCIPLES TO ACTION

Just about anyone can focus on meaningful actions every once in a while, particularly after profound moments of insight. But lasting transformation is the result of consistent, ongoing, and daily practice. In this chapter, we learned how to align our being with our doing. We also learned about common pitfalls that occur when trying to shift our habit energy. We discussed the value of selectively watering seeds of groundedness via small, simple, and specific actions. We examined how intentionally designing our surroundings in a way that promotes those actions is more effective than relying on sheer force of will. We explored concrete plans to water each seed not just in formal practice but in everyday life, and considered the exponential power of undertaking this journey with the support of others.

The next and final chapter circles back to why adopting the principles of groundedness is so vital, for both individuals and society as a whole. We'll also see how when it comes to realizing a more grounded kind of success there is no destination. The path is the goal and the goal is the path. The urgent, imperative, and at times difficult task is simply to stay on it.

9

FOCUS ON THE PROCESS, LET THE OUTCOMES TAKE CARE OF THEMSELVES

The stakes are high. Heroic individualism and its related discontents—burnout, restlessness, anxiety, depression, loneliness, and addiction—won't change if we keep doing what we've been doing. We need a new approach, a better way. Adopting and practicing the principles of groundedness is just that. We must do what we can to create lives that we are fully involved in—lives in which we cultivate acceptance, presence, patience, vulnerability, deep community, and movement. Ancient wisdom, modern science, and the experience of people who consistently prioritize groundedness show how these principles work in combination to underpin a happy, healthy, fulfilling, and truly successful life.

Focusing on groundedness will, at least at times, be challenging. Regularly practicing the principles in this book requires overcoming both personal and cultural inertia. The fact that neglecting one's foundational ground is so common in today's world says a lot more about today's world than it does about the principles in this book.

Groundedness is most effective and rewarding when it is embarked upon as an ongoing practice. As with any other practice, there will be highs and lows, good days and bad days. You'll have periods of strong motivation when everything is clicking. And you'll have periods when you relapse into old ways of being and doing. All of this is normal. "The way practice works," an anonymous Japanese Zen teacher once remarked, "is that we build up our practice, then it falls apart. And then we build it up again, and then it falls apart again. This is the way it goes."

This final chapter offers a transformative new way to think about successful practice—both how to build it up and what to do when it falls apart. Equipped with this knowledge, you'll be ready to fully embark on the path of living a more grounded life.

REDEFINING PRACTICE

When you first hear the word *practice*, what comes to mind? Perhaps you think of an athlete executing drills between games, or a musician playing scales on a piano to prepare for a recital. This is how I thought about practice for a long time. But working on this book got me thinking about it in a much broader way. Practice means approaching an endeavor deliberately, with care, and with the intention to continually grow. It requires paying close attention to the feedback you receive—both internal and from external sources you trust—and adjusting accordingly.

You can have a writing practice, a legal practice, a medical practice, a running practice, a parenting practice, a leadership practice, a coaching practice, a teaching practice, an artistic practice, or a meditation practice. The art of practice is applicable to anything in which you strive to advance, whether that means shaving two minutes off your marathon time, improving your public speaking, or becoming a stronger, kinder, wiser, and more grounded person. When an activity becomes a practice, it shifts from something that you are doing at a point in time to an ongoing process of becoming. James Carse, a professor of history and religion at New York University, called this kind of practice an "infinite game." In his underground classic *Finite and Infinite Games*, Carse writes that a finite game is one that will be won or lost, that will come to a definite end. An infinite game, however, as its name suggests, is ongoing. The whole purpose is to keep playing.

Viewing something as an isolated activity lends itself to "good" and "bad" judgments, forgetfulness, and discontinuity. Viewing something as a practice lends itself to continual learning, meaningful change, and integration. When you consider a pursuit as a practice, you still have acute ups and downs. But they are merely part of a larger process—and it is the larger process that matters. Not the outcome of that process, but how you go about the process itself. Outcomes are short-lived and ephemeral. More than 99 percent of life is the process.

In his book *A New Republic of the Heart*, philosopher Terry Patten writes that life satisfaction is largely a by-product of transitioning from being a *seeker*, or someone who wants a certain lifestyle, to a *practitioner*, or someone who lives that lifestyle. Echoing major themes of the being-doing cycle, Patten writes, "A whole life of regular, ongoing practice is necessary. . . . We are always reinforcing the neural circuits associated with what we are doing right now. . . . Whatever way we are being, we're more likely to be that way in the future. *This means we are always practicing something.*"

Any significant change requires significant practice. As you begin emphasizing groundedness in your life, keep the following points in mind, all of which have been alluded to in prior chapters and can serve as guiding principles for successful practice.

- Do not worry about achieving a specific result. Focus on being where you are and applying the principles of groundedness to the best of your ability *right now.* If you concentrate on the process, the results you are hoping for tend to take care of themselves.

- Bring intentionality to everything you do. Keep coming back to the principles of groundedness and your actions for living them out. There is much about life that you cannot control, but there is also plenty that you can. Concentrate on the latter.

- Work with like-minded people whenever possible, and don't be scared to ask for help when you need it. Asking for help is not a sign of weakness; it is a sign of strength.

- Take a long view and assume you will fail every now and again. If you expect occasional failures they won't surprise you or throw you off course. They simply become part of the process, information that you can learn from and that will help you grow.

- Contrary to the cultural norms of heroic individualism, do not compare yourself to others. Compare yourself to prior versions of yourself and judge yourself based on the effort you are exerting in the present moment.

Eastern wisdom traditions conceptualize practice as a path—*tao* in Chinese and *do* in Japanese. This represents the never-ending, infinite nature of practice. There is no destination, just continual learning and refining, truly an infinite game. Conceiving of the practice of groundedness in this way allows for the inevitability that sometimes you will veer off the path. That's fine. Your work is to get back on.

GETTING BACK ON THE PATH

Here is a common trap that so many people, including me, fall into: reading a book like this one, having a clear sense of the changes they'll make, making those changes and feeling great, and then experiencing a failure (or series of failures) and imploding completely. Every part of this cycle is inevitable except the last part. I've never met someone who made a meaningful change and did not experience failure. It is not whether you fail but how you react to failure that is a vital component of successful change. Anyone can feel inspired and motivated. Anyone can get started and stick with the program when things are going well. But few can bounce back from failure. This is not merely speculation. Every year there is a large and representative sample of people attempting change that shows us this is true. The University of Scranton, a small Jesuit school in Scranton, Pennsylvania, tracks the success rate of New Year's resolutions. Their data show that over 40 percent of people who make a New Year's resolution will have blown it off by February. And 90 percent of people will have fallen off by the end of the year. This is not because people are soft. It's because changing your lifestyle is hard.

I suspect one reason people fail with New Year's resolutions is because they assume that they need to be perfect, and they become frustrated with themselves when they are not. The harder the change, the more likely you are to fail or relapse into old ways of being. Your reaction when this happens is critical. If you completely let yourself off the hook (*Screw it. I guess this just wasn't for me.*) you can expect a bad outcome. But the flip side is also true. If your inner voice is overly harsh and judgmental (*How come I still can't get this right? I'm no good!*) the failure or relapse is only likely to compound.

A 2012 study published in the *Personality and Social Psychology Bulletin* found that individuals who react to failure with self-compassion get back on the bandwagon more swiftly than those who judge themselves harshly. For the study, Juliana Breines and Serena Chen, researchers at the University of California, Berkeley, had participants reflect on personal weaknesses and then manipulated situations so that participants would experience failure. The participants who were taught self-compassion skills felt better about overcoming their weaknesses and reacted to failure by leaning in instead of leaning out or quitting. "These findings suggest that, somewhat paradoxically, taking an accepting approach to personal failure may make people more motivated to improve themselves," write Breines and Chen.

The work of another psychologist, Kristin Neff, an associate professor at the University of Texas, shows that if you judge yourself for messing up, you are liable to feel guilt or shame, and it is often this guilt or shame that prevents you from bouncing back and continuing down the path. A theme across all of Neff's research is that being <u>kind to yourself in the midst of struggle and hardship gives you the</u> <u>resilience that you need to thrive</u>. The best occasion to do what you wanted to do may have been yesterday, but the second-best occasion is today. Beating yourself up is a complete waste of time and energy.

Conventional wisdom on behavior change asserts that on one extreme there is taking responsibility and picking oneself up by the bootstraps, and on the other there is showing oneself boundless love and caring. While these are often pitted against each other, the truth is that they are complementary; you need both. <u>You need</u> <u>to marry strong self-discipline with strong self-compassion</u>. We discussed the importance of applying self-compassion in chapter 2, but it is worth coming back to here. The self-compassion practices are useful for approaching the journey of transitioning to a more grounded life as a whole:

- Stop shoulding all over yourself.

- Treat your failures and the judgmental voice in your head as you would treat a crying baby.

- Develop a mantra to interrupt negative thought cycles and help get you back on the path: *This is what is happening right now* or *I am doing the best I can.**

---

*For additional detail, see pages 49 to 51, where we discussed all of these practices at length.

A woman I've worked with for some time now named Lauren is a C-suite leader at a large and fast-growing technology company. She was one of the first employees. Now her company has over six hundred employees and everyone else on the founding team has moved on, making Lauren the oldest person (not in age—she's only in her thirties—but in tenure) at her company. She is an incredible person and leader. Her biggest challenge is that she cares, and sometimes too much. She feels like the company is her baby, and that it's on her to shepherd it into the future. Yes, in our coaching sessions we work on all the principles of groundedness, but perhaps more than anything we work on self-compassion.

The poet T. S. Eliot famously wrote, "Teach us to care and not to care." It wasn't in Lauren's nature to do the latter. She got to a point in her skyrocketing career where it wasn't her head—she's impeccably sharp and rational—that was getting in the way of her feeling solid, strong, and fulfilled. It was her heart. She had to soften up a bit, which can be particularly hard for women leaders, who are sometimes wrongly profiled as soft to begin with. Using the aforementioned practices, Lauren learned to let herself feel all her emotions—and then do the hard work of creating space to hold them so she wouldn't be overtaken by them. Once she married her disciplined, questioning, and rational mind with a softer and more spacious heart, she became a more grounded and unstoppable leader. More important, she became a healthier and more grounded person.

MIND AND HEART

One of the most popular Eastern mantras is *Om mani padme hum*. The Sanskrit is roughly translated to English as "the jewel in the lotus." While it has many meanings, the psychologist and Buddhist teacher Jack Kornfield offers the following explanation of its symbolism: "Compassion arises when the jewel of the mind rests in the lotus of the heart."

In the West, we tend to separate the mind and the heart. The mind thinks rationally. It knows hard and objective truths. It judges good from bad, right from wrong. The heart is emotional and soft. If we pay too close attention to it, it will make us weak or lead us astray. But the truth lies outside this dichotomy altogether. The mind is most powerful when it is situated in the heart, when striving and trying to get something right is held with love and compassion. As Kornfield writes, and as Lauren experienced, the mind in the heart gains "a diamond-like clarity." Hence the jewel in the lotus.

If we—you, me, anyone—are to be successful in transitioning to a grounded life, we'd be wise to situate our minds in our hearts. We need to recognize and see clearly when we veer off the path. And we need to show ourselves the understanding and kindness required to get back on—again and again and again. Until we attempt to apply them, the principles of groundedness are completely intellectual, nice and tidy in our minds. But the real world is messy. Putting into practice the life-changing lessons of this book depends on our heart space every bit as much as on our head space.

Stay on the path. Fall off the path. Get back on the path. It's as simple and as hard as that.

Conclusion

Heading into the year 2021, as I finish writing this book, COVID-19 continues to ravage much of the world. At the same time, across America and Europe massive demonstrations for social justice have taken hold. While these events seem especially significant—and they are—they are not the first wave of change and disruption in our lifetime, and they certainly won't be the last. What these events are doing, however, is making people step back and ask: *What do I stand for? How do I want to live? What do I want to do with my short time on this earth?* Whether you are reading this book in 2021 or 2051, these are questions we should always be asking. They are perennial.

In the preceding pages, I've argued that the type of conventional success we spend so much time and energy chasing—money, fame, relevance, busyness, followers—isn't all it's cracked up to be. It is not that we shouldn't ever strive. It is that we should spend more time and energy focusing on the deep, internal foundation—the ground—from which any and all striving emerges. Once we do this, our definition of success changes, and so does the texture of our drive to succeed and the satisfaction of experiencing it. We still have the chance to reach great heights, but we do so from a more solid ground. We feel better. We perform better. And we become better community members, too. Consider this: in his iconic novel *Brave New World*, Aldous Huxley presented a dystopian picture of what happens when people are controlled by invisible forces that prey on their psyche. Superficial thrills lead to the dullest of lives, and the loss of independent thinking, purpose, and anything remotely close to depth precipitates the erosion of society. We are not living in *Brave New World* . . . yet. But we are certainly getting too close for comfort. The time to push back is now. Living out the principles of groundedness is every bit as much a civic action as it is an individual one.

My hope is that this book has given you a new way to think about how you want to live your life. And that it's also given you the practices to actualize it. To choose acceptance over delusion and wishful thinking. To choose presence over distraction. To choose patience over speed. To choose vulnerability over invincibility. To choose community over isolation. To choose movement over sitting still. To choose groundedness over heroic individualism.

Living a grounded life may start as a personal project, but groundedness spreads and grows in communities. If you found this book valuable, please share it with your family, friends, neighbors, and colleagues. The more of us who take on this project together, the better.

Acknowledgments

Publishing this book was a team effort. I am filled with gratitude for everyone involved.

First, I'd like to thank all my coaching clients (whose names have been changed) for allowing me to accompany them on their respective paths. It is a privilege working with these individuals. I learn as much from them as I teach. I'd also like to thank all the other people whose stories I told. I appreciate you being so raw and vulnerable with me and, in some cases, with the greater public. In particular, I'd like to thank Steven Hayes, Sarah True, Mike Posner, and Andrea Barber for opening up to me in detail about some of your most harrowing moments.

Next, I'd like to thank my inner circle—the people who are there for me day in and day out, through thick and thin. I don't know what or where I'd be without you. My collaborator Steve

Magness. My friend Justin Bosley. My brother, Eric Stulberg. And my therapist and coach, Brooke Van Oosbree. I love all of you.

I'd also like to thank a few specific colleagues, mentors, and friends who had a direct impact on this book. My psychiatrist, Lucas Van Dyke, for diagnosing me with OCD and helping me to better understand and heal my mind. Judson Brewer, my meditation teacher, for showing me how to pay deep attention. Ryan Holiday and Cal Newport for encouraging me to write this book, and to write it with Portfolio. David Epstein for being my sounding board on pretty much everything (the man truly does have range). Liana Imam for multiple conversations and reads, and for so generously sharing her wealth of literary skill. Adam Alter for listening to me describe the concepts in this book ad infinitum and remarking, ever so subtly, "I think the word you are looking for is *grounded.*" Mario Fraioli for miles upon miles of hiking and conversations about "success," conversations that became the genesis of this book. Shalane Flanagan, not only for letting me share her story but also for our close friendship. Rich Roll and Emily Esfahani Smith for being friends, thought partners, and coconspirators when it comes to redefining how the culture thinks about success. The members of my daily email group not already mentioned: Mike Joyner, Christie Aschwanden, Alex Hutchinson, Jonathan Wai, Amby Burfoot—you all make me smarter by osmosis, even if it's virtual. Adam Grant, Kelly McGonigal, and Dan Pink for always encouraging me to write, write, write—and books! Toby Bilanow for editing my essays and giving me precious real estate in *The New York Times*, where I first explored some of the ideas in this book. Matt Skenazy and Wes Judd for being my longtime editors at *Outside* magazine. I am so proud of the work we've done together. We set out to make a difference in how people conceive health, well-being, and performance—and we did. Kelly Starrett, Brett Bartholomew, and Zach Greenwald for teaching me so much about physical movement. Bob Kocher for being a wonderful mentor and friend. And last but not least, thanks to my good friends Jason Dizik and Brandon Rennels for endless conversations on the topics in this book.

Next up are people whose work helps me make sense of myself, many of whom I haven't even met. Yet their imprint is on me, and thus on my work. The writers and teachers Mark Epstein, Thich Nhat Hanh, George Leonard, Tara Brach, Erich Fromm, Robert Pirsig, Richard Rohr, Jon Kabat-Zinn, Joseph Goldstein, Jack Kornfield, Leslie Jamison, and David Whyte. The musicians Sara Bareilles, Trevor Hall, the Avett Brothers, Benjamin Haggerty, and Mike Posner.

Now on to those who have been in the publishing trenches with me. Ted Weinstein, for helping me to start my career as an author. Laurie Abkemeier, for being the best agent, coach, and all-around literary thought partner. Writing for Laurie feels like playing basketball for Phil Jackson. She's simply the best. To the entire team at Portfolio, for believing in this book from day one: My publisher, Adrian Zackheim, who listened to me explain the idea, said, "I get it," and then enthusiastically encouraged his team to make this book a reality. My editor Niki Papadopoulos, who pushed me in all the best ways and made this book so much better. When I turned in my first draft Niki told me, "This is very good—here's what will make it great . . ." I listened to her, and she was right. Leah

Trouwborst, for pushing the manuscript across the finish line and leading the process on creative packaging, which resulted in a title and subtitle that I think is pretty rad (not an easy feat!). Kym Surridge, Will Jeffries, Karen Ninnis, and Katie Hurley, for catching all my errors and helping to make the writing shine. To Kimberly Meilun, for coordinating all the moving pieces. And to Tara Gilbride and her marketing team for doing everything possible to help this book reach readers everywhere.

I want to thank my parents for raising me with solid values and my in-laws for being supportive always.

Above all, thanks to my best friend and life partner, Caitlin (also my primary editor). I am so fortunate to be in this infinite game with you. I love you. And thanks to my son, Theo—there are no words.

Recommended Reading

During my thinking, writing, and refining process for *The Practice of Groundedness*, I had all of the following books on a shelf directly above my desk. I referred to them repeatedly, and I'm sure I will continue to in the future. All of these books have greatly influenced how I think, write, coach, and live. I am grateful they exist. What follows is a list of recommended reading, sorted by chapter. Like the principles of groundedness, many of these books complement each other. Although sorting in this way is not perfect, it was the best option.

1: GROUNDED TO SOAR

- *In the Buddha's Words* by Bhikkhu Bodhi
- *The Heart of the Buddha's Teaching* by Thich Nhat Hanh
- *Selected Writings: Discourses and Selected Writings* by Epictetus

- *Meditations* by Marcus Aurelius
- *A Guide to the Good Life* by William Irvine
- *Tao Te Ching* by Lao-tzu (translated by Stephen Mitchell)
- *Letters from a Stoic* by Seneca
- *The Nicomachean Ethics* by Aristotle
- *The Hidden Life of Trees* by Peter Wohlleben
- *The True Believer* by Eric Hoffer
- *How to Live: A Life of Montaigne* by Sarah Bakewell
- *The Path* by Michael Puett and Christine Gross-Loh
- *The Sane Society* by Erich Fromm

2: ACCEPT WHERE YOU ARE TO GET YOU WHERE YOU WANT TO GO

- *Radical Acceptance* by Tara Brach
- *The Hero with a Thousand Faces* by Joseph Campbell
- *A Liberated Mind* by Steven Hayes
- *After the Ecstasy, the Laundry* by Jack Kornfield
- *On Becoming a Person* by Carl Rogers
- *The Recovering* by Leslie Jamison
- *Going to Pieces Without Falling Apart* by Mark Epstein
- *Almost Everything: Notes on Hope* by Anne Lamott

3: BE PRESENT SO YOU CAN OWN YOUR ATTENTION AND ENERGY

- *Full Catastrophe Living* by Jon Kabat-Zinn
- *Deep Work* and *Digital Minimalism* by Cal Newport
- *Mindfulness in Plain English* by Bhante Gunaratana
- *Mindfulness* by Joseph Goldstein
- *The Craving Mind* by Judson Brewer
- *Irresistible* by Adam Alter
- *The Inner Game of Tennis* by W. Timothy Gallwey
- *To Have or to Be?* by Erich Fromm
- *The Art of Loving* by Erich Fromm
- *Devotions* by Mary Oliver
- *Flow* by Mihaly Csikszentmihalyi
- *Stillness Is the Key* by Ryan Holiday
- *The Wisdom of Insecurity* by Alan Watts
- *Zen and the Art of Motorcycle Maintenance* by Robert Pirsig
- *Lila* by Robert Pirsig
- *Amusing Ourselves to Death* by Neil Postman
- *The Shallows* by Nicholas Carr

4: BE PATIENT AND YOU'LL GET THERE FASTER

- *Crossing the Unknown Sea* by David Whyte
- *Mastery* by George Leonard

- *The Way of Aikido* by George Leonard
- *Range* by David Epstein

5: EMBRACE VULNERABILITY TO DEVELOP GENUINE STRENGTH AND CONFIDENCE

- *Consolations* by David Whyte
- *The Heart Aroused* by David Whyte
- *Sounds Like Me* by Sara Bareilles
- *No Mud, No Lotus* by Thich Nhat Hanh
- *Rising Strong* by Brené Brown
- *Braving the Wilderness* by Brené Brown
- *The Fearless Organization* by Amy Edmondson
- *Teaming* by Amy Edmondson
- *Rilke on Love* by Rainer Maria Rilke

6: BUILD DEEP COMMUNITY

- *Tribe* by Sebastian Junger
- *Friendship* by Lydia Denworth
- *Middlemarch* by George Eliot
- *Escape from Freedom* by Erich Fromm
- *Suicide* by Émile Durkheim
- *Deacon King Kong* by James McBride

7: MOVE YOUR BODY TO GROUND YOUR MIND

- *Spark* by John Ratey
- *The Joy of Movement* by Kelly McGonigal
- *The Ultimate Athlete* by George Leonard

8: FROM PRINCIPLES TO ACTION

- *Falling Upward* by Richard Rohr
- *The Glass Bead Game* by Hermann Hesse
- *The Art of Living* by Thich Nhat Hanh
- *Wherever You Go, There You Are* by Jon Kabat-Zinn
- *Becoming Wise* by Krista Tippett

9: FOCUS ON THE PROCESS, LET THE OUTCOMES TAKE CARE OF THEMSELVES

- *A New Republic of the Heart* by Terry Patten
- *The Life We Are Given* by George Leonard and Michael Murphy
- *Brave New World* by Aldous Huxley

Notes

1: GROUNDED TO SOAR

8 **After I wrote about my experience with OCD:** Brad Stulberg, "When a Stress Expert Battles Mental Illness," *Outside*, March 7, 2018, https://www.outside online.com/2279856/anxiety-cant-be-trained-away.

9 **The groundbreaking sociologist Émile Durkheim:** Émile Durkheim, *Suicide: A Study in Sociology* (Snowball Press, 2012; originally published in French in 1897), 252–53.

9 **Rates of clinical anxiety and depression:** National Institute of Mental Health, "Mental Health Information: Statistics," https://www.nimh.nih.gov/health /statistics/index.shtml.

9 **Addictions to harmful substances:** National Institute on Alcohol Abuse and Alcoholism, "Alcohol Facts and Statistics," https://www.niaaa.nih.gov /publications/brochures-and-fact-sheets/alcohol-facts-and-statistics; US National Library of Medicine, "Opioid Addiction," MedlinePlus, https://ghr .nlm.nih.gov/condition/opioid-addiction#statistics.

9 **That is the highest this number:** "Pain in the Nation: The Drug, Alcohol and Suicide Crises and Need for a National Resilience Strategy," Trust for America's Health, https://www.tfah.org/report-details/pain-in-the-nation/.

10 **The data "suggests a trend":** Mary Caffrey, "Gallup Index Shows US Well-being Takes Another Dip," *AJMC*, February 27, 2019, https://www.ajmc.com /newsroom/gallup-index-shows-us-wellbeing-takes-another-dip-.

10 **Even prior to the COVID-19 pandemic:** Jeffrey M. Jones, "U.S. Church Membership Down Sharply in Past Two Decades," Gallup, April 18, 2019, https://news.gallup.com/poll/248837/church-membership-down-sharply-past -two-decades.aspx.

10 **At the same time, experts believe:** Julianne Holt-Lunstad, "The Potential Public Health Relevance of Social Isolation and Loneliness: Prevalence, Epidemiology, and Risk Factors," *Public Policy & Aging Report* 27, no. 4 (2017): 127–30, https://academic.oup.com/ppar/article/27/4/127/4782506.

10 **In 2019, the World Health Organization classified burnout:** Ben Wigert and Sangeeta Agrawal, "Employee Burnout, Part 1: The 5 Main Causes," Gallup, July 12, 2018, https://www.gallup.com/workplace/237059/employee-burnout -part-main-causes.aspx; "Burn-out an 'Occupational Phenomenon': International Classification of Diseases," World Health Organization, May 28, 2019, https://www.who.int/mental_health/evidence/burn-out/en/.

10 **Insomnia is more common than ever:** Pradeep C. Bollu and Harleen Kaur, "Sleep Medicine: Insomnia and Sleep," *Missouri Medicine* 116, no. 1 (2019): 68–75, https://www.ncbi.nlm.nih.gov/pmc/articles/PMC6390785/; James Dahlhamer et al., "Prevalence of Chronic Pain and High-Impact Chronic Pain Among Adults—United States, 2016," *Morbidity and Mortality Weekly Report* 67, no. 36 (2018): 1001–6, https://www.cdc.gov/mmwr/volumes/67/wr /mm6736a2.htm.

14 **Instead, happiness is found in the present moment:** Robb B. Rutledge et al., "A Computational and Neural Model of Momentary Subjective Well-being," *PNAS* 111, no. 33 (2014): 12252–57, http://www.pnas.org/content/111/33 /12252.full.

14 **But research conducted by the Nobel Prize–winning economnist Daniel Kahneman:** Daniel Kahneman and Angus Deaton, "High Income Improves Evaluation of Life but Not Emotional Well-being," *PNAS* 107, no. 38 (2010): 16489–93, https://www.pnas.org/content/107/38/16489.

15 **Ben-Shahar says that if the cycle of seeking happiness:** A. C. Shilton, "You Accomplished Something Great. So Now What?" *New York Times*, May 28, 2019, https://www.nytimes.com/2019/05/28/smarter-living/you-accomplished -something-great-so-now-what.html.

17 **Buddhism also teaches a concept called "right effort":** Bhikkhu Bodhi, ed., *In the Buddha's Words: An Anthology of Discourses from the Pali Canon* (Somerville, MA: Wisdom Publications, 2005), 239.

17 **"The deeper and lower the ground":** Meister Eckhart, *Selected Writings*, trans. Oliver Davies (London, UK: Penguin Books, 1994), 45.

19 **"And I think that when you anchor":** Seth Simons, "The New Formula for Personal Fulfillment," *Fatherly*, October 12, 2018, https://www.fatherly.com /love-money/the-new-formula-for-personal-fulfillment/.

23 **"If you want to garden":** Thich Nhat Hanh, *The Heart of the Buddha's Teaching: Transforming Suffering into Peace, Joy, and Liberation* (New York: Harmony Books, 1999), 42.

2: ACCEPT WHERE YOU ARE

26 "My body failed me": Karen Rosen, "After Rio Heartbreak, Triathlete Sarah True 'Ready to Rumble' into New Season," Team USA, March 2, 2017, https:// www.teamusa.org/News/2017/March/02/After-Rio-Heartbreak-Triathlete -Sarah-True-Ready-To-Rumble-Into-New-Season.

29 "The curious paradox": See Carl R. Rogers, *On Becoming a Person: A Therapist's View of Psychotherapy* (New York: Mariner Books, 1995).

32 "While the Danes are very satisfied": Kaare Christensen, Anne Maria Herskind, and James W. Vaupel, "Why Danes Are Smug: Comparative Study of Life Satisfaction in the European Union," *BMJ* 333 (2006): 1289, http:// www.bmj.com/content/333/7582/1289.

32 They found that "momentary happiness": Rutledge et al., "A Computational and Neural Model of Momentary Subjective Well-being."

32 "I think it often wrings the joy": Jason Fried, "Living Without Expectations," *Signal v Noise* (blog), March 8, 2017, https://m.signalvnoise.com/living -without-expectations-1d66adb10710.

32 "The crux of the curious difficulty": Joseph Campbell, *The Hero with a Thousand Faces*, 3rd ed. (Novato, CA: New World Library, 2008), 101.

33 He's written forty-four books: "Highly Cited Researchers (h>100) According to Their Google Scholar Citations Public Profiles," Ranking Web of Universities, accessed July 2020, http://www.webometrics.info/en/node/58.

36 But, as Hayes's work and my own experience: See Steven C. Hayes, *A Liberated Mind: How to Pivot Toward What Matters* (New York: Avery, 2020), for a summary of this body of work.

36 Hayes will be the first: "316: Steven C. Hayes on Developing Psychological Flexibility," in *The One You Feed*, hosted by Eric Zimmer, podcast, January 21, 2020, https://www.oneyoufeed.net/psychological-flexibility/.

37 "And for a human being to feel stress is normal": Marcus Aurelius, *Meditations* (London, UK: Penguin Books, 2005), 76.

37 Epictetus, another revered Stoic: Epictetus, *Discourses and Selected Writings* (London, UK: Penguin Books, 2008), 180–81.

39 "Just as the Buddha willingly opened himself up": Tara Brach, *Radical Acceptance: Embracing Your Life with the Heart of a Buddha* (New York: Bantam Books, 2004), 61.

41 Research out of the University of Kent in England: Joachim Stoeber, Mark A. Uphill, and Sarah Hotham, "Predicting Race Performance in Triathlon: The Role of Perfectionism, Achievement Goals, and Personal Goal Setting," *Journal of Sport and Exercise Psychology* 31, no. 2 (2009): 211–45, https://repository .canterbury.ac.uk/download/c447b55ea3ec0148c05f2c0754c0527ef311a1f30d7 ce8c8ca7cda6f70348f10/277408/Uphill_2009_%5B1%5D.pdf.

41 A study published in the *Journal of Sport and Exercise Psychology*: Andrew J. Elliot et al., "Achievement Goals, Self-Handicapping, and Performance

Attainment: A Mediational Analysis," *Journal of Sport and Exercise Psychology* 28, no. 3 (2006): 344–61, https://journals.humankinetics.com/doi/abs/10.1123 /jsep.28.3.344.

41 **Other studies show that while fear:** David E. Conroy, Jason P. Willow, and Jonathan N. Metzler, "Multidimensional Fear of Failure Measurement: The Performance Failure Appraisal Inventory," *Journal of Applied Sport Psychology* 14, no. 2 (2002): 76–90, https://psycnet.apa.org/record/2002-13632-002.

41 **"Nothing I accept about myself":** Audre Lorde, *Sister Outsider: Essays and Speeches* (New York: Crossing Press, 1984).

42 **As you'll see in the following examples:** Craig Smith, "COVID-19 Update from Dr. Smith: 3/29/20," Columbia Surgery, https://columbiasurgery.org /news/covid-19-update-dr-smith-32920.

47 **The meditation teacher Michele McDonald:** Tara Brach, "Feeling Overwhelmed? Remember RAIN," *Mindful*, February 7, 2019, https://www .mindful.org/tara-brach-rain-mindfulness-practice/.

47 **physical pain:** David M. Perlman et al., "Differential Effects on Pain Intensity and Unpleasantness of Two Meditation Practices," *Emotion* 10, no. 1 (2010): 65–71, https://www.ncbi.nlm.nih.gov/pmc/articles/PMC2859822/.

47 **emotional pain:** UMass Memorial Health Care Center for Mindfulness, https://www.umassmed.edu/cfm/research/publications/.

47 **social anxiety:** Philippe R. Goldin and James J. Gross, "Effects of Mindfulness-Based Stress Reduction (MBSR) on Emotion Regulation in Social Anxiety Disorder," *Emotion* 10, no. 1 (2010): 83–91, https://www.ncbi .nlm.nih.gov/pmc/articles/PMC4203918/.

47 **making difficult decisions:** Igor Grossman and Ethan Kross, "Exploring Solomon's Paradox: Self-Distancing Eliminates the Self-Other Asymmetry in Wise Reasoning About Close Relationships in Younger and Older Adults," *Psychological Science* 25, no. 8 (2014): 1571–80, https://pdfs.semanticscholar .org/799a/d44cb6d51bbf6c14ef8e83d6dc74d083f2af.pdf.

48 **Studies conducted at the University of California, Berkeley:** Özlem Ayduk and Ethan Kross, "From a Distance: Implications of Spontaneous Self-Distancing for Adaptive Self-Reflection," *Journal of Personality and Social Psychology* 98, no. 5 (2010): 809–29, https://www.ncbi.nlm.nih.gov/pmc /articles/PMC2881638/.

49 **If, on the other hand, you can muster up kindness:** Juliana G. Breines and Serena Chen, "Self-Compassion Increases Self-Improvement Motivation," *Personality and Social Psychology Bulletin* 38, no. 9 (2012): 1133–43, http://cite seerx.ist.psu.edu/viewdoc/download?doi=10.1.1.362.5856&rep=rep1&type=pdf.

49 **"What progress have I made?"** Seneca, *Letters from a Stoic* (London, UK: Penguin Books, 1969), 14.

51 **Research shows that mantras:** Ephrat Livni, "To Get Better at Life, Try This Modern Mantra," *Quartz*, May 8, 2019, https://t.co/biGWjp3tBs.

52 **Long-standing psychological research:** For thinking: Daniel M. Wegner et al.,

"Paradoxical Effects of Thought Suppression," *Journal of Personality and Social Psychology* 53, no. 1 (1987): 5–13, http://psycnet.apa.org/record/1987-33493-001; and for feeling: Jutta Joormann and Ian H. Gotlib, "Emotion Regulation in Depression: Relation to Cognitive Inhibition," *Cognition and Emotion* 24, no. 2 (2010): 281–98, https://www.ncbi.nlm.nih.gov/pmc/articles/PMC2839199/.

54 **"In a sense, if we try to control a situation":** Judson Brewer, *The Craving Mind: From Cigarettes to Smartphones to Love—Why We Get Hooked and How We Can Break Bad Habits* (New Haven, CT: Yale University Press, 2017), 111.

55 **As Bud Winter, widely regarded:** Bud Winter and Jimson Lee, *Relax and Win: Championship Performance in Whatever You Do* (2012).

3: BE PRESENT

58 **Thousands of years ago, the Stoic philosopher Seneca:** Seneca, *On the Shortness of Life*, trans. C. D. N. Costa (New York: Penguin Books, 2005), 96.

58 **Researchers at the University of Michigan:** "Multitasking: Switching Costs," American Psychological Association, March 20, 2006, https://www.apa.org/research/action/multitask.aspx.

58 **This is twice the decrease one experiences:** Jim Sollisch, "Multitasking Makes Us a Little Dumber," *Chicago Tribune*, August 10, 2010, https://www.chicagotribune.com/opinion/ct-xpm-2010-08-10-ct-oped-0811-multitask-20100810-story.html.

59 **"A wandering mind," the researchers write:** Steve Bradt, "Wandering Mind Not a Happy Mind," *Harvard Gazette*, November 11, 2010, https://news.harvard.edu/gazette/story/2010/11/wandering-mind-not-a-happy-mind/.

60 **Research from the United Kingdom's telecom regulator:** *Communications Market Report*, Ofcom, August 2, 2018, https://www.ofcom.org.uk/__data/assets/pdf_file/0022/117256/CMR-2018-narrative-report.pdf.

60 **Other research shows that 71 percent of people:** "Americans Don't Want to Unplug from Phones While on Vacation, Despite Latest Digital Detox Trend," press release, Asurion, May 17, 2018, https://www.asurion.com/about/press-releases/americans-dont-want-to-unplug-from-phones-while-on-vacation-despite-latest-digital-detox-trend/.

61 **Each and every notification we get:** See: Adam Alter, "What Is Behavioral Addiction and Where Did It Come From?" in *Irresistible: The Rise of Addictive Technology and the Business of Keeping Us Hooked* (New York: Penguin Press, 2017).

61 **Everything about the apps we check on our phones:** Susana Martinez-Conde and Stephen L. Macknik, "How the Color Red Influences Our Behavior," *Scientific American*, November 1, 2014, https://www.scientificamerican.com/article/how-the-color-red-influences-our-behavior/.

NOTES

61 **In his book *Riveted*:** Jim Davies, *Riveted: The Science of Why Jokes Make Us Laugh, Movies Make Us Cry, and Religion Makes Us Feel One with the Universe* (New York: Palgrave Macmillan, 2014), 91, 175.

62 **In 1951, writing in *The Wisdom of Insecurity*:** Alan Watts, *The Wisdom of Insecurity: A Message for an Age of Anxiety* (New York: Vintage Books, 2011), 21.

62 **In *The Art of Living*:** Thich Nhat Hanh, *The Art of Living* (New York: HarperOne, 2017), 147.

64 **Studies show that merely having these potential distractions:** Bill Thornton et al., "The Mere Presence of a Cell Phone May Be Distracting: Implications for Attention and Task Performance," *Social Psychology* 45, no. 6 (2014): 479–88, https://metacog2014-15.weebly.com/uploads/3/9/2/9/39293965/thornton _faires_robbins_y_rollins_in_press_presence_cell_phone_distracting.pdf.

65 **"It is not that we have a short time to live":** Seneca, *Shortness of Life*, 1–4.

66 **A critical precondition for flow:** Mihaly Czikszentmihalyi, *Flow: The Psychology of Optimal Experience* (New York: Harper Perennial, 2008).

66 **The Stoics wrote:** Seneca, *Letters From a Stoic*, 26.

67 **"How often our minds leave the present":** Bradt, "Wandering Mind Not a Happy Mind."

67 **The results of their study:** Matthew A. Killingsworth and Daniel T. Gilbert, "A Wandering Mind Is an Unhappy Mind," *Science* 330, no. 6006 (2010): 932, http://www.danielgilbert.com/KILLINGSWORTH%20&%20GILBERT %20(2010).pdf.

68 **"The 75 years and 20 million dollars spent":** Scott Stossel, "What Makes Us Happy, Revisited," *Atlantic*, May 2013, https://www.theatlantic.com/magazine /archive/2013/05/thanks-mom/309287/.

68 **When we are fully present, we enter a sacred space:** George Leonard, *Mastery: The Keys to Success and Long-Term Fulfillment* (New York: Plume, 1992), 40.

69 **It wasn't long before the song spread:** Billboard, "Mike Posner, 'Cooler Than Me,'" Chart History, https://www.billboard.com/music/Mike-Posner/chart -history/HBU/song/644778.

69 **Posner—who as a child worried his parents:** Quotation is a lyric from the Mike Posner song "Come Home" on the album *Keep Going*.

71 **In the middle of the video:** Mike Posner, "Naughty Boy, Mike Posner—Live Before I Die," November 14, 2019, music video, 4:02, https://youtu.be /uXeZNXdu-gs.

72 **When he was setting out on his walk:** Mike Posner (@MikePosner), Twitter status, May 29, 2019, https://twitter.com/MikePosner/status/113374382932 2948608?s=20.

73 **His productive activity relies on a foundation:** Erich Fromm, *The Art of Loving* (New York: HarperPerennial, 2006), 101.

73 **Research increasingly shows that what is important:** Ayelet Fishbach, Ronald S. Friedman, and Arie W. Kruglanski, "Leading Us Not unto Temptation:

Momentary Allurements Elicit Overriding Goal Activation," *Journal of Personality and Social Psychology* 84, no. 2 (2003): 296–309.

81 **"Your work is simply seeing and letting go":** Jon Kabat-Zinn, *Full Catastrophe Living: Using the Wisdom of Your Body and Mind to Face Stress, Pain, and Illness,* rev. ed. (New York: Bantam Books, 2013), 443.

81 **"Distractions are really paper tigers":** Bhante Gunaratana, *Mindfulness in Plain English* (Somerville, MA: Wisdom Publications, 2011), 119.

81 **Studies show that attention is like a muscle:** "How the Internet May Be Changing the Brain," *Neuroscience News,* June 5, 2019, https://t.co/rUgy7hPkJg.

83 **Though the exact date is unknown:** Wumen Huikai, author quotes, Great Thoughts Treasury, http://www.greatthoughtstreasury.com/author/author-209.

85 **"How we spend our days":** Annie Dillard, quotes, Goodreads, https://www.goodreads.com/quotes/530337-how-we-spend-our-days-is-of-course-how-we.

4: BE PATIENT

90 **Research conducted by the firm Forrester:** "Akamai Reveals 2 Seconds as the New Threshold of Acceptability for Ecommerce Web Page Response Times," Akamai, September 14, 2009, https://www.akamai.com/us/en/about/news/press/2009-press/akamai-reveals-2-seconds-as-the-new-threshold-of-acceptability-for-ecommerce-web-page-response-times.jsp.

90 **There's no reason to believe:** Steve Lohr, "For Impatient Web Users, an Eye Blink Is Just Too Long to Wait," *New York Times,* February 29, 2012, http://www.nytimes.com/2012/03/01/technology/impatient-web-users-flee-slow-loading-sites.html.

90 **The author Nicholas Carr:** Teddy Wayne, "The End of Reflection," *New York Times,* June 11, 2016, http://www.nytimes.com/2016/06/12/fashion/internet-technology-phones-introspection.html?_r=0.

90 **A prescient 2012 report:** Janna Anderson and Lee Rainie, "Millennials Will Benefit and Suffer Due to Their Hyperconnected Lives," Pew Research Center, February 29, 2012, https://www.pewresearch.org/internet/2012/02/29/millennials-will-benefit-and-suffer-due-to-their-hyperconnected-lives/.

92 **Writing about these and other experimental nutrition results:** Aaron E. Carroll, "What We Know (and Don't Know) About How to Lose Weight," *New York Times,* March 26, 2018, https://www.nytimes.com/2018/03/26/upshot/what-we-know-and-dont-know-about-how-to-lose-weight.html.

93 **Though the ship set sail in 1831:** *Britannica,* s.v. "Charles Darwin," https://www.britannica.com/biography/Charles-Darwin/The-Beagle-voyage.

93 **In his own words:** "Charles Darwin," NNDB.com, https://www.nndb.com/people/569/000024497/.

95 **On a cellular level:** Martin J. MacInnis and Martin J. Gibala, "Physiological

Adaptations to Interval Training and the Role of Exercise Intensity," *Journal of Physiology* 595, no. 9 (2017): 2915–30, https://www.ncbi.nlm.nih.gov/pmc /articles/PMC5407969/.

95 **A 2018 study published in the prestigious journal** *Nature*: Lu Liu et al., "Hot Streaks in Artistic, Cultural, and Scientific Careers," *Nature* 559 (2018): 396–99, https://www.nature.com/articles/s41586-018-0315-8.

96 **Vincent van Gogh produced more than twenty paintings:** Jessica Hallman, "Hot Streak: Finding Patterns in Creative Career Breakthroughs," *Penn State News*, September 6, 2018, https://news.psu.edu/story/535062/2018/09/06 /research/hot-streak-finding-patterns-creative-career-breakthroughs.

96 **From 1996 to 2008, he bounced:** Jeff Stein, "Ta-Nehisi Coates's Advice to Young Journalists: Get Off Twitter," *Vox*, December 21, 2016, https://www.vox .com/policy-and-politics/2016/12/21/13967504/twitter-young-journalists-coates.

96 **the** *Times* **called Coates:** Concepción de León, "Ta-Nehisi Coates and the Making of a Public Intellectual," *New York Times*, September 29, 2017, https:// www.nytimes.com/2017/09/29/books/ta-nehisi-coates-we-were-eight-years-in -power.html.

96 **Speaking to young writers:** Stein, "Ta-Nehisi Coates's Advice to Young Journalists."

97 **"It's not really that mystical":** *The Atlantic*, "Creative Breakthroughs: Ta-Nehisi Coates," interview, September 27, 2013, video, 1:15, https://www.youtube.com /watch?v=6voLZDYgPzY&feature=emb_title.

97 **"I want to stress the importance of being young:** Steven Kotler, "Is Silicon Valley Ageist or Just Smart?" *Forbes*, February 14, 2015, https://www.forbes .com/sites/stevenkotler/2015/02/14/is-silicon-valley-ageist-or-just-smart /#1e987d17ed65.

98 **Even those who start their companies:** Jake J. Smith, "How Old Are Successful Tech Entrepreneurs?" KelloggInsight, May 15, 2018, https://insight .kellogg.northwestern.edu/article/younger-older-tech-entrepreneurs.

101 **Kipchoge told** *The New York Times* **that he rarely:** Scott Cacciola, "Eliud Kipchoge Is the Greatest Marathoner, Ever," *New York Times*, September 14, 2018, https://www.nytimes.com/2018/09/14/sports/eliud-kipchoge-marathon .html.

101 **His coach, Patrick Sang:** Ed Caesar, "The Secret to Running a Faster Marathon? Slow Down," *Wired*, February 8, 2017, https://www.wired .com/2017/02/nike-two-hour-marathon-2/.

101 **"To be precise, I am just going to try":** Cacciola, "Eliud Kipchoge Is the Greatest Marathoner, Ever."

102 **"We must distinguish happiness from excitement":** Thich Nhat Hanh, *The Art of Power* (New York: HarperOne, 2007), 81.

104 **It was developed in the early 1950s:** "The Collected Works of D. W. Winnicott," Oxford Clinical Psychology, https://www.oxfordclinicalpsych.com/page/599.

106 **But according to the Taoist scholar Stephen Mitchell:** Stephen Mitchell, *Tao Te Ching: A New English Version* (New York: Harper Perennial, 2006), foreword, i.

106 **The master, wrote Lao-tzu:** Mitchell, *Tao Te Ching*, 63.

106 **They found that overemphasizing goals:** Lisa D. Ordóñez et al., "Goals Gone Wild: The Systematic Side Effects of Over-Prescribing Goal Setting" (working paper, Harvard Business School, 2009), http://www.hbs.edu/faculty /Publication%20Files/09-083.pdf.

109 **When acute workload:** Tim J. Gabbett, "The Training–Injury Prevention Paradox: Should Athletes Be Training Smarter *and* Harder?" *British Journal of Sports Medicine* 50, no. 5 (2016): 273–80, http://bjsm.bmj.com/content/early /2016/01/12/bjsports-2015-095788.

113 **Rohitassa said:** This particular translation of the story comes from Thich Nhat Hanh's *The Art of Living*, 84.

5: EMBRACE VULNERABILITY

120 **"In all my research's two-hundred-thousand-plus pieces of data":** Brené Brown, *Braving the Wilderness: The Quest for True Belonging and the Courage to Stand Alone* (New York: Random House, 2019), 146.

121 **"Vulnerability is not a weakness":** David Whyte, *Consolations: The Solace, Nourishment and Underlying Meaning of Everyday Words* (Langley, WA: Many Rivers Press, 2015), Audible audio ed., 4 hours, 2 minutes.

121 **"I want to unfold":** Rainer Maria Rilke, *Rilke's Book of Hours: Love Poems to God*, trans. Anita Barrows and Joanna Macy (New York: Riverhead Books, 2005).

122 **research published in the journal** *Archives of General Psychiatry*: Ronald C. Kessler et al., "The Epidemiology of Panic Attacks, Panic Disorder, and Agoraphobia in the National Comorbidity Survey Replication," *Archives of General Psychiatry* 63, no. 4 (2006): 415–24, https://www.ncbi.nlm.nih.gov /pubmed/16585471.

122 **Yet a small number go on to develop:** "Any Anxiety Disorder," National Institute of Mental Health, https://www.nimh.nih.gov/health/statistics /prevalence/any-anxiety-disorder-among-adults.shtml.

122 **Writing in** *The Players' Tribune*: Kevin Love, "Everyone Is Going Through Something," *Players' Tribune*, March 6, 2018, https://www.theplayerstribune .com/en-us/articles/kevin-love-everyone-is-going-through-something.

123 **shooting guard DeMar DeRozan:** DeMar DeRozan (@DeMar_DeRozan), Twitter post, February 17, 2018, https://twitter.com/DeMar_DeRozan /status/964818383303688197?s=20.

124 **"It's one of them things":** Doug Smith, "Raptors' DeRozan Hopes Honest Talk on Depression Helps Others," *The Star* (Toronto), February 26, 2018, https://

www.thestar.com/sports/raptors/2018/02/25/raptors-derozan-hopes-honest
-talk-on-depression-helps-others.html.

125 **In Greek mythology, the god Pan:** Campbell, *The Hero with a Thousand Faces*,
66–68.

125 **"In my heart of hearts":** Sara Bareilles, "Sara Bareilles Shows Her
Vulnerabilities on New Album, 'Amidst the Chaos,'" interview by Robin
Young, *Here & Now*, WBUR, radio broadcast, April 4, 2019, https://www
.wbur.org/hereandnow/2019/04/04/sara-bareilles-amidst-the-chaos.

125 **She says that the more she is:** Sara Bareilles, *Sounds Like Me: My Life (So Far)
in Song* (New York: Simon & Schuster, 2015), 40.

127 **Intellectual humility is associated:** Mark R. Leary et al., "Cognitive and
Interpersonal Features of Intellectual Humility," *Personality and Social Psychology
Bulletin* 43, no. 6 (2017): 793–813, https://journals.sagepub.com/doi/abs/10
.1177/0146167217697695.

127 **In her memoir:** Bareilles, *Sounds Like Me*, 39.

128 **It is believed that these "vulnerable apes":** Nick P. Winder and Isabelle C.
Winder, "Complexity, Compassion and Self-Organisation: Human Evolution
and the Vulnerable Ape Hypothesis," *Internet Archaeology* 40 (2015), https://
www.researchgate.net/publication/277940624_Complexity_Compassion_and
_Self-Organisation_Human_Evolution_and_the_Vulnerable_Ape_Hypothesis.

128 **On day two or three:** "Baby's First 24 Hours," Pregnancy, Birth and Baby,
https://www.pregnancybirthbaby.org.au/babys-first-24-hours.

130 **In the fourth century BC:** Mitchell, *Tao Te Ching*, 8.

131 **As you might guess:** Amy C. Edmondson, *The Fearless Organization: Creating
Psychological Safety in the Workplace for Learning, Innovation, and Growth*
(Hoboken, NJ: John Wiley & Sons, 2019).

131 **"All of us are vulnerable":** Amy Edmondson (@AmyCEdmondson), Twitter
post, February 7, 2020, https://twitter.com/AmyCEdmondson/status
/1225830003453124608?s=20.

133 **Emotional flexibility is essential:** Todd B. Kashdan, "Psychological Flexibility
as a Fundamental Aspect of Health," *Clinical Psychology Review* 30, no. 7
(2010): 865–78, https://www.ncbi.nlm.nih.gov/pmc/articles/PMC2998793/.

135 **DeMar DeRozan says that his mom:** Smith, "Raptors' DeRozan Hopes Honest
Talk on Depression Helps Others."

6: BUILD DEEP COMMUNITY

140 **the rate of loneliness in America:** Elizabeth Bernstein, "When Being Alone
Turns into Loneliness, There Are Ways to Fight Back," *Wall Street Journal*,
November 4, 2013, http://www.wsj.com/articles/SB10001424052702303936904
579177700699367092.

NOTES

140 **Other research, conducted by AARP:** Knowledge Networks and Insight Policy Research, *Loneliness Among Older Adults: A National Survey of Adults 45+* (Washington, DC: AARP, 2010), https://assets.aarp.org/rgcenter/general /loneliness_2010.pdf.

140 **A poll conducted in 2018:** "New Cigna Study Reveals Loneliness at Epidemic Levels in America," Cigna, May 1, 2018, https://www.cigna.com/newsroom /news-releases/2018/new-cigna-study-reveals-loneliness-at-epidemic-levels-in -america.

141 **Loneliness is associated:** F. M. Alpass and S. Neville, "Loneliness, Health and Depression in Older Males," *Aging & Mental Health* 7, no. 3 (2003): 212–16, https://www.tandfonline.com/doi/abs/10.1080/1360786031000101193.

141 **Researchers from Brigham Young University:** Julianne Holt-Lunstad, Timothy B. Smith, and J. Bradley Layton, "Social Relationships and Mortality Risk: A Meta-analytic Review," *PLOS Medicine* 7, no. 7 (2010).

141 **"We are asking one person":** London Real, "Esther Perel on Society & Marriage," interview with Brian Rose, July 14, 2015, video, 5:08, https://www .youtube.com/watch?v=X9HiXw8Pmbo.

142 **"Humans don't mind hardship":** Sebastian Junger, *Tribe: On Homecoming and Belonging* (New York: Twelve, 2016), introduction, 17.

143 **When one or more of these basic needs:** Edward L. Deci and Richard M. Ryan, "Self-Determination Theory," in P. A. M. Van Lange, A. W. Kruglanski, and E. T. Higgins, eds., *Handbook of Theories of Social Psychology* (London, UK: Sage Publications, 2012), 416–36, https://psycnet.apa.org/record/2011-21800-020.

143 **But not so for someone in a group:** Jonathan Haidt, *The Righteous Mind: Why Good People Are Divided by Politics and Religion* (New York: Vintage, 2013), 102.

144 **A 2003 study out of the University of California, Los Angeles:** Joan B. Silk, Susan C. Alberts, and Jeanne Altmann, "Social Bonds of Female Baboons Enhance Infant Survival," *Science* 302, no. 5648 (2003): 1231–34, https://www .ncbi.nlm.nih.gov/pubmed/14615543.

144 **Baboons who were socially isolated:** Joan B. Silk et al., "Strong and Consistent Social Bonds Enhance the Longevity of Female Baboons," *Current Biology* 20, no. 15 (2010): 1359–61, https://www.ncbi.nlm.nih.gov/pubmed/20598541; Elizabeth A. Archie et al., "Social Affiliation Matters: Both Same-Sex and Opposite-Sex Relationships Predict Survival in Wild Female Baboons," *Proceedings of the Royal Society B: Biological Sciences* 281, no. 1793 (2014), https:// www.ncbi.nlm.nih.gov/pubmed/25209936.

144 **"To feel completely alone and isolated":** Erich Fromm, *Escape from Freedom* (New York: Farrar and Rinehart, 1941), 16–17.

145 **If someone becomes chronically lonely:** John T. Cacioppo and William Patrick, *Loneliness: Human Nature and the Need for Social Connection* (New York: W. W. Norton, 2008).

146 **Cacioppo induced loneliness in college students:** John T. Cacioppo et al., "Loneliness Within a Nomological Net: An Evolutionary Perspective," *Journal*

of Research in Personality 40 (2006): 1054–85, https://static1.squarespace.com /static/539a276fe4b0dbaee772658b/t/53b0e963e4b0d621f6aaa261/1404103 011411/8_10.1016_CacioppoHawkleyBurleson.pdf.

146 **the brains of lonely people were continually scanning for threats:** Stephanie Cacioppo et al., "Loneliness and Implicit Attention to Social Threat: A High-Performance Electrical Neuroimaging Study," *Cognitive Neuroscience* 7, no. 1–4 (2016): 138–59, https://www.tandfonline.com/doi/abs/10.1080/1758892 8.2015.1070136.

147 **In book eight of his** *Confessions***:** Saint Augustine, *Confessions*, trans. R. S. Pine-Coffin (London, UK: Penguin, 1961), Book 8.

147 **"I could not be happy without friends":** Saint Augustine, *Confessions*, 101.

147 **In a famous sermon:** Saint Augustine, *Works of Saint Augustine*, trans. Edmund Hill, OP, John E. Rotelle (New York: New City Press, 1991), Sermon 299.

147 **In a passage appearing in the Pali Canon:** Bodhi, *In the Buddha's Words*.

148 **Olds and Schwartz explain:** Jacqueline Olds and Richard S. Schwartz, *The Lonely American: Drifting Apart in the Twenty-first Century* (Boston: Beacon Press, 2009).

148 **"The dynamic of friendship":** David Whyte, *Crossing the Unknown Sea: Work as a Pilgrimage of Identity* (New York: Riverhead, 2001).

149 **French sociologist Émile Durkheim observed:** Durkheim, *Suicide*, 209.

151 **In 2020, that number is close to 70 percent:** Andrew Perrin and Monica Anderson, "Share of U.S. Adults Using Social Media, Including Facebook, Is Mostly Unchanged Since 2018," Pew Research Center, April 10, 2019, https:// www.pewresearch.org/fact-tank/2019/04/10/share-of-u-s-adults-using-social -media-including-facebook-is-mostly-unchanged-since-2018/.

151 **Writing in her 2020 book:** Lydia Denworth, *Friendship: The Evolution, Biology, and Extraordinary Power of Life's Fundamental Bond* (New York: W. W. Norton, 2020), 166.

152 **Overall, the effect of social media on relationships:** J. T. Hancock et al., "Social Media Use and Psychological Well-being: A Meta-analysis," 69th Annual International Communication Association Conference, Washington, DC, 2019.

152 **"You get very small advantages for your well-being":** Lydia Denworth, "Worry over Social Media Use and Well-being May Be Misplaced," *Psychology Today*, May 30, 2019, https://www.psychologytoday.com/us/blog/brain-waves/201905 /worry-over-social-media-use-and-well-being-may-be-misplaced.

152 **They reviewed data on more than 350,000 adolescents:** Amy Orben and Andrew K. Przybylski, "The Association Between Adolescent Well-being and Digital Technology Use," *Nature Human Behaviour* 3 (2019): 173–82, https:// www.nature.com/articles/s41562-018-0506-1?mod=article_inline.

152 **association between social media use and adolescent well-being:** Robbie Gonzalez, "Screens Might Be as Bad for Mental Health as . . . Potatoes," *Wired*,

January 14, 2019, https://www.wired.com/story/screens-might-be-as-bad-for
-mental-health-as-potatoes/.

152 **a study conducted at the University of Pittsburgh:** Brian A. Primack et al.,
"Social Media Use and Perceived Social Isolation Among Young Adults in the
U.S.," *American Journal of Preventive Medicine* 53, no. 1 (2017): 1–8, https://
www.ncbi.nlm.nih.gov/pubmed/28279545.

153 **Studies show that presence and physical touch:** Pavel Goldstein, Irit
Weissman-Fogel, and Simone G. Shamay-Tsoory, "The Role of Touch in
Regulating Inter-partner Physiological Coupling During Empathy for Pain,"
Scientific Reports 7 (2017): 3252, https://www.nature.com/articles/s41598-017
-03627-7.

153 **"If you use those [digital] connections as a way station":** Olga Khazan, "How
Loneliness Begets Loneliness," *Atlantic*, April 6, 2017, https://www.theatlantic
.com/health/archive/2017/04/how-loneliness-begets-loneliness/521841/.

154 **research shows that babies do not bond as well:** Sarah Myruski et al., "Digital
Disruption? Maternal Mobile Device Use Is Related to Infant Social-Emotional
Functioning," *Developmental Science* 21, no. 4 (2018): e12610, https://dennis
-tiwary.com/wp-content/uploads/2017/10/Myruski_et_al-2017
-Developmental_Science_Still-Face.pdf.

154 **"If the only acceptance you can get of yourself":** Olga Khazan, "How to Break
the Dangerous Cycle of Loneliness," CityLab, April 6, 2017, https://www
.bloomberg.com/news/articles/2017-04-06/john-cacioppo-explains-the
-psychology-of-loneliness.

155 **"[When someone's] body, mind, and soul are his capital":** Erich Fromm, *The
Sane Society* (New York: Henry Holt and Company, 1955).

155 **Studies reveal that if you bear witness:** Jean Decety and William Ickes, eds.,
The Social Neuroscience of Empathy (Cambridge, MA: MIT Press, 2009), https://
psycnet.apa.org/record/2009-02253-000.

156 **"When we witness what happens to others":** Kim Armstrong, "'I Feel Your
Pain': The Neuroscience of Empathy," Association for Psychological Science,
December 29, 2017, https://www.psychologicalscience.org/observer/i-feel-your
-pain-the-neuroscience-of-empathy.

156 **They found that when someone became happy or sad:** James H. Fowler and
Nicholas A. Christakis, "Dynamic Spread of Happiness in a Large Social
Network: Longitudinal Analysis over 20 Years in the Framingham Heart
Study," *BMJ* 337 (2008): a2338, https://www.bmj.com/content/337/bmj.a2338.

156 **Another study, aptly titled "I'm Sad You're Sad":** Jeffrey T. Hancock et al.,
"I'm Sad You're Sad: Emotional Contagion in CMC" (Proceedings of the 2008
ACM Conference on Computer Supported Cooperative Work, San Diego,
November 8–12, 2008), http://collablab.northwestern.edu/CollabolabDistro
/nucmc/p295-hancock.pdf.

156 **Emotions like happiness, sadness, and anger spread:** Adam D. I. Kramer,
Jamie E. Guillory, and Jeffrey T. Hancock, "Experimental Evidence of

Massive-Scale Emotional Contagion Through Social Networks," *PNAS* 111, no. 24 (2014): 8788–90, https://www.pnas.org/content/111/24/8788.

157 **If someone is working in the same room as others:** Ron Friedman et al., "Motivational Synchronicity: Priming Motivational Orientations with Observations of Others' Behaviors," *Motivation and Emotion* 34, no. 1 (2010): 34–38, https://www.researchgate.net/publication/225164928_Motivational _synchronicity_Priming_motivational_orientations_with_observations_of _others%27_behaviors.

157 **A 2017 study out of Northwestern University:** "Sitting Near a High-Performer Can Make You Better at Your Job," Kellogg Insight, May 8, 2017, https:// insight.kellogg.northwestern.edu/article/sitting-near-a-high-performer-can -make-you-better-at-your-job.

157 **"Shalane Flanagan Effect":** Lindsay Crouse, "How the 'Shalane Flanagan Effect' Works," *New York Times*, November 11, 2017, https://www.nytimes .com/2017/11/11/opinion/sunday/shalane-flanagan-marathon-running .html#:~:text=.

159 **One of Cacioppo's first principles:** Khazan, "How to Break the Dangerous Cycle of Loneliness."

160 **When helping others, the part of your brain:** Brad Stulberg and Steve Magness, *Peak Performance: Elevate Your Game, Avoid Burnout, and Thrive with the New Science of Success* (New York: Rodale, 2017), 157–90.

160 **"Tending to others is as natural":** Shelley E. Taylor, *The Tending Instinct: Women, Men, and the Biology of Our Relationships* (New York: Times Books, 2002), 153–65.

160 **Studies show that volunteering is associated:** Jerf W. K. Yeung, Zhuoni Zhang, and Tae Yeun Kim, "Volunteering and Health Benefits in General Adults: Cumulative Effects and Forms," *BMC Public Health* 18 (2018): 8, https://www .ncbi.nlm.nih.gov/pmc/articles/PMC5504679/.

160 **Volunteering may be especially powerful:** Randee B. Bloom, "Role Identity and Demographic Characteristics as Predictors of Professional Nurse Volunteerism" (PhD diss., Capella University, 2012), https://pqdtopen.proquest .com/doc/962412634.html?FMT=ABS.

160 **This is precisely why the American Association of Retired Persons:** "Create the Good," AARP, https://createthegood.aarp.org/.

161 **The 2018 American Family Survey:** "Religious Landscape Study," Pew Research Center, https://www.pewforum.org/religious-landscape-study /generational-cohort/.

161 **A 2016 study published in *JAMA Internal Medicine*:** Shanshan Li et al., "Association of Religious Service Attendance with Mortality Among Women," *JAMA Internal Medicine* 176, no. 6 (2016): 777–85, https://jamanetwork.com /journals/jamainternalmedicine/fullarticle/2521827.

161 **A 2017 study published in the journal:** Marino A. Bruce et al., "Church Attendance, Allostatic Load and Mortality in Middle Aged Adults," *PLOS One*

12, no. 5 (2017): e0177618, https://journals.plos.org/plosone/article?id=10.1371/journal.pone.0177618.

162 **A species designed "where all must cooperate":** Peter Sterling, *What Is Health? Allostasis and the Evolution of Human Design* (Cambridge, MA: MIT Press, 2020), 102.

163 **This is why support groups:** Kathlene Tracy and Samantha P. Wallace, "Benefits of Peer Support Groups in the Treatment of Addiction," *Substance Abuse and Rehabilitation* 7 (2016): 143–54, https://www.ncbi.nlm.nih.gov/pmc/articles/PMC5047716/.

166 **As Aristotle wrote:** Aristotle, *The Nicomachean Ethics*, Oxford World Classic's Version (Oxford University Press, 2009).

166 **"If you consort with someone covered in dirt":** Epictetus, *Discourses and Selected Writings* (New York: Penguin Classics, 2008).

168 **Catmull suggests a few guiding principles:** Ed Catmull with Amy Wallace, *Creativity, Inc.: Overcoming the Unseen Forces That Stand in the Way of True Inspiration* (New York: Random House, 2014), 86–106.

169 **The Zen master Thich Nhat Hanh teaches:** Hanh, *The Heart of the Buddha's Teaching*, 124–27.

169 **"In my tradition we learn":** Thich Nhat Hanh, "What Is Sangha?" *Lion's Roar*, July 7, 2017, https://www.lionsroar.com/the-practice-of-sangha/.

7: MOVE YOUR BODY

173 **A 2019 analysis out of King's College London:** Felipe Barreto Schuch and Brendon Stubbs, "The Role of Exercise in Preventing and Treating Depression," *Current Sports Medicine Reports* 18, no. 8 (2019): 299–304, http://journals.lww.com/acsm-csmr/Fulltext/2019/08000/The_Role_of_Exercise_in_Preventing_and_Treating.6.aspx#O3-6.

173 **Other research has found similar effects:** Brett R. Gordon et al., "The Effects of Resistance Exercise Training on Anxiety: A Meta-analysis and Meta-regression Analysis of Randomized Controlled Trials," *Sports Medicine* 47, no. 12 (2017): 2521–32, https://www.ncbi.nlm.nih.gov/pubmed/28819746.

173 **They found that between 40 and 50 percent:** Felipe B. Schuch et al., "Exercise as a Treatment for Depression: A Meta-analysis Adjusting for Publication Bias," *Journal of Psychiatric Research* 77 (2016): 42–51, https://www.ashlandmhrb.org/upload/exercise_as_a_treatment_for_depression_-_a_meta-analysis_adjusting_for_publication_bias.pdf.

173 **Researchers from the University of Limerick in Ireland:** Gordon et al., "Effects of Resistance Exercise Training on Anxiety."

174 **In the 1640s, French philosopher René Descartes:** David Cunning, ed., *The Cambridge Companion to Descartes' Meditations* (Cambridge, UK: Cambridge University Press, 2014), 279.

175 **physical activity has the opposite effect:** Y. Netz et al., "The Effect of a Single Aerobic Training Session on Cognitive Flexibility in Late Middle-Aged Adults," *International Journal of Sports Medicine* 28, no. 1 (2007): 82–87, http://www.ncbi.nlm.nih.gov/pubmed/17213965.

176 **Evelyn Stevens:** Brad Stulberg, "How Exercise Shapes You, Far Beyond the Gym," The Growth Equation, https://thegrowtheq.com/how-exercise-shapes-you-far-beyond-the-gym/.

176 **A study published in the *British Journal of Health Psychology*:** Megan Oaten and Ken Cheng, "Longitudinal Gains in Self-Regulation from Regular Physical Exercise," *British Journal of Health Psychology* 11, pt. 4 (2006): 717–33, http://www.ncbi.nlm.nih.gov/pubmed/17032494.

177 **Another study, this one published:** Birte von Haaren et al., "Does a 20-Week Aerobic Exercise Training Programme Increase Our Capabilities to Buffer Real-Life Stressors? A Randomized, Controlled Trial Using Ambulatory Assessment," *European Journal of Applied Physiology* 116, no. 2 (2016): 383–94, http://www.ncbi.nlm.nih.gov/pubmed/26582310.

178 **For exercisers to experience flow:** Pirkko Markula, "Exercise and 'Flow,'" *Psychology Today*, January 11, 2013, https://www.psychologytoday.com/us/blog/fit-femininity/201301/exercise-and-flow.

178 **movement is a "keystone habit":** Charles Duhigg, *The Power of Habit: Why We Do What We Do in Life and Business* (New York: Random House, 2014).

182 **A growing body of research:** Arran Davis, Jacob Taylor, and Emma Cohen, "Social Bonds and Exercise: Evidence for a Reciprocal Relationship," *PLOS One* 10, no. 8 (2015): e0136705, https://journals.plos.org/plosone/article?id=10.1371/journal.pone.0136705.

182 **In her book *The Joy of Movement*:** Kelly McGonigal, *The Joy of Movement: How Exercise Helps Us Find Happiness, Hope, Connection, and Courage* (New York: Avery, 2019).

182 **Exercise scientists refer to this as "muscular bonding":** McGonigal, *The Joy of Movement*.

182 **"Like any nature-harnessing phenomenon":** McGonigal, *The Joy of Movement*.

184 **A 2019 study by the Centers for Disease Control and Prevention:** Roland Sturm and Deborah A. Cohen, "Free Time and Physical Activity Among Americans 15 Years or Older: Cross-Sectional Analysis of the American Time Use Survey," *Preventing Chronic Disease* 16 (2019), https://www.cdc.gov/pcd/issues/2019/19_0017.htm.

185 **The participants who took the short walk:** Marily Oppezzo and Daniel L. Schwartz, "Give Your Ideas Some Legs: The Positive Effect of Walking on Creative Thinking," *Journal of Experimental Psychology: Learning, Memory, and Cognition* 40, no. 4 (2014): 1142–52, https://www.apa.org/pubs/journals/releases/xlm-a0036577.pdf.

185 **The great irony is that so many schools:** Centers for Disease Control and Prevention, *The Association Between School-Based Physical Activity, Including*

Physical Education, and Academic Performance (Atlanta: U.S. Department of Health and Human Services, 2010), https://www.cdc.gov/healthyyouth/health _and_academics/pdf/pa-pe_paper.pdf.

185 **The effect is so powerful:** J. Eric Ahlskog et al., "Physical Exercise as a Preventive or Disease-Modifying Treatment of Dementia and Brain Aging," *Mayo Clinic Proceedings* 86, no. 9 (2011): 876–84, http://www .mayoclinicproceedings.org/article/S0025-6196(11)65219-1/abstract.

186 **"Physical fitness and brain performance are tied together":** Aishwarya Kumar, "The Grandmaster Diet: How to Lose Weight While Barely Moving," ESPN, September 13, 2019, https://www.espn.com/espn/story/_/id/27593253 /why-grandmasters-magnus-carlsen-fabiano-caruana-lose-weight-playing-chess.

188 **A meta-analysis that reviewed thirteen studies:** Edward R. Laskowski, "What Are the Risks of Sitting Too Much?" Mayo Clinic, https://www.mayoclinic .org/healthy-lifestyle/adult-health/expert-answers/sitting/faq-20058005.

188 **Other studies show that even if you exercise:** Peter T. Katzmarzyk et al., "Sitting Time and Mortality from All Causes, Cardiovascular Disease, and Cancer," *Medicine and Science in Sports and Exercise* 41, no. 5 (2009): 998–1005, https://www.flexchair.nl/wp-content/uploads/sites/12/2017/05/sitting_time _and_mortality_from_all_causes.pdf.

188 **A study published in the** *Journal of the American Heart Association*: Gretchen Reynolds, "Those 2-Minute Walk Breaks? They Add Up," *New York Times*, March 28, 2018, https://www.nytimes.com/2018/03/28/well/move/walking -exercise-minutes-death-longevity.html.

189 **The researchers concluded that while all movement:** Audrey Bergouignan et al., "Effect of Frequent Interruptions of Prolonged Sitting on Self-Perceived Levels of Energy, Mood, Food Cravings and Cognitive Function," *International Journal of Behavioral Nutrition and Physical Activity* 13, no. 113 (2016), http:// ijbnpa.biomedcentral.com/articles/10.1186/s12966-016-0437-z.

192 **"Whether it is a stroll on a sunny day":** Emmanuel Stamatakis, Mark Hamer, and Marie H. Murphy, "What Hippocrates Called 'Man's Best Medicine': Walking Is Humanity's Path to a Better World," *British Journal of Sports Medicine* 52, no. 12 (2018): 753–54, https://bjsm.bmj.com/content/52/12/753.

193 **"A very simple way to grasp a 'brisk' pace":** Emmanuel Stamatakis et al., "Self-Rated Walking Pace and All-Cause, Cardiovascular Disease and Cancer Mortality: Individual Participant Pooled Analysis of 50,225 Walkers from 11 Population British Cohorts," *British Journal of Sports Medicine* 52, no. 12 (2018): 761–68, https://bjsm.bmj.com/content/52/12/761.

193 **Another 2019 study:** Alpa V. Patel et al., "Walking in Relation to Mortality in a Large Prospective Cohort of Older U.S. Adults," *American Journal of Preventive Medicine* 54, no. 1 (2018): 10–19, https://pubmed.ncbi.nlm.nih.gov/29056372/.

194 **Though experts believe running:** Julia Belluz, "Should You Walk or Run for Exercise? Here's What the Science Says," *Vox*, November 25, 2017, https:// www.vox.com/2015/8/4/9091093/walking-versus-running; "Running Injuries," Yale Medicine, https://www.yalemedicine.org/conditions/running-injury/#.

194 "Above all, do not lose your desire to walk": Søren Kierkegaard, *The Laughter Is on My Side: An Imaginative Introduction to Kierkegaard*, ed. Roger Poole and Henrik Stangerup (Princeton, NJ: Princeton University Press, 1989).

196 Research from Japan: Yoshifumi Miyazaki et al., "Preventive Medical Effects of Nature Therapy," *Nihon Eiseigaku Zasshi* 66, no. 4 (2011): 651–56, https://www.ncbi.nlm.nih.gov/pubmed/21996763 [article in Japanese].

196 Other research, out of Stanford University: Gregory N. Bratman et al., "Nature Experience Reduces Rumination and Subgenual Prefrontal Cortex Activation," *PNAS* 112, no. 28 (2015): 8567–72, http://www.pnas.org/content/early/2015/06/23/1510459112.full.pdf.

8: FROM PRINCIPLES TO ACTION

206 "It is not that we should abandon, neglect, or deny": Meister Eckhart, *Selected Writings*, 45.

214 He wrote this down and published it: Maxwell Maltz, *Psycho-Cybernetics, Deluxe Edition: The Original Text of the Classic Guide to a New Life* (New York: TarcherPerigee, 2016).

214 Some people took just eighteen days: Phillippa Lally et al., "How Are Habits Formed: Modelling Habit Formation in the Real World," *European Journal of Social Psychology* 40, no. 6 (2010): 998–1009, https://onlinelibrary.wiley.com/doi/abs/10.1002/ejsp.674.

214 "Habit energy is stronger than we are": Thich Nhat Hanh, "Dharma Talk: Transforming Negative Habit Energies," *Mindfulness Bell*, Summer 2000, https://www.mindfulnessbell.org/archive/2015/12/dharma-talk-transforming-negative-habit-energies.

215 It shows that relying on willpower alone: Roy F. Baumeister, Dianne M. Tice, and Kathleen D. Vohs, "The Strength Model of Self-Regulation: Conclusions from the Second Decade of Willpower Research," *Perspectives on Psychological Science* 13, no. 2 (2018): 141–45, https://www.ncbi.nlm.nih.gov/pubmed/29592652.

217 The work of Stanford researcher BJ Fogg: "BJ Fogg," *Armchair Expert*, hosted by Dax Shepard, podcast, March 5, 2020, https://armchairexpertpod.com/pods/bj-fogg.

219 If you're doing a task to please someone: For more, see Michelle Segar, *No Sweat: How the Simple Science of Motivation Can Bring You a Lifetime of Fitness* (New York: AMACOM, 2015).

9: FOCUS ON THE PROCESS

231 In his underground classic: James P. Carse, *Finite and Infinite Games: A Vision of Life as Play and Possibility* (New York: Free Press, 2013).

NOTES

231 **"A whole life of regular, ongoing practice":** Terry Patten, *A New Republic of the Heart* (Berkeley, CA: North Atlantic Books, 2018).

234 **Their data show that over 40 percent:** "New Years Resolution Statistics," Statistic Brain Research Institute, https://www.statisticbrain.com/new-years -resolution-statistics/.

234 **"These findings suggest that, somewhat paradoxically":** Breines and Chen, "Self-Compassion Increases Self-Improvement Motivation."

235 **A theme across all of Neff's research:** Kristin Neff and Christopher Germer, *The Mindful Self-Compassion Workbook: A Proven Way to Accept Yourself, Build Inner Strength, and Thrive* (New York: Guilford Press, 2018).

237 **the psychologist and Buddhist teacher Jack Kornfield:** "The Mind and the Heart," JackKornfield.com, https://jackkornfield.com/mind-heart/.

Index

INDEX

INDEX